The Coming of Aging

Learning to Live from the Inside Out

by
Jean Deitch Shula

PublishAmerica
Baltimore

ISBN: 1-4241-2553-7
PUBLISHED BY PUBLISHAMERICA, LLLP
www.publishamerica.com
Baltimore

Printed in the United States of America

Contents

Introduction

When I announced to my family and friends that I was taking a year-long sabbatical to learn to take direction from the *voice within,* to practice living from the inside out, the responses were kindly placating. "What a novel idea," was accompanied with eye rolling humor. When I announced that I was closing my psychotherapy practice and resigning from the hospice I had co-founded, their faces reflected some alarm and quite a bit of interest. "Has she finally flipped?" When I continued by telling them that I was renting my house and selling my Saab to buy a used camper to go rambling around the country for a year on my own, the responses became volatile.

From outright admiration to fearful prognosis for my untimely demise, everyone weighed in with an opinion about my vulnerability as a fifty-something woman traveling alone in the world with only dependence on the Holy Spirit for company. "Are you crazy? It must be *the Change!*"

Evidently it was okay to push the parameters a bit with self-help books on how to change my life or to join a drumming group that met on the beach every full moon; but honestly, who in her right mind believed my plan was practical or safe? *The Coming of Aging: Learning to Live from the Inside Out* is my chronicle of what turned out to be a wondrous, practical, mystical year despite the sincere forebodings of those who were concerned about me.

As is true of most journeys, this one started months in advance. I practiced daily the awesomely sacred notion that the divine not only abides in us all, but is waiting…waiting…for us to quiet the clamoring of the deafening outside voices long enough to listen in the silence to our own profoundly willing inner voice. In other words, I practiced the practical applications of taking direction from the inside out.

I learned far more from my journey than I could ever have imagined when I headed out. The journey became much deeper than my need for a change. It became a trip into awareness, a trip into all the bits and pieces that make me *me*. Wow. It was then I knew that the journey was my understanding of what it means to be at the time of life when I accepted that I could no longer fool myself. I was at the cusp of the coming of aging.

Do any of us know the exact moment when we segued from adolescence into adulthood? Most of us were too busy living it to have the perspicacity to observe it. It is only in retrospect that we tell our coming of age stories, sometimes with laughter and sometimes with awful embarrassment. We have not the consciousness nor the inclination at most stages of development to say, "Ah yes, yesterday I went from adulthood to mid-life." In fact, in our culture, it is popular never to admit that one is growing into maturity. Imagine the surprise when I knew for the first time in fifty-three years that I was actually in the stew of the coming of aging. I was conscious of my own developmental process, and what a gift it was!

Learning the ebb and flow of the internal and external is a deeply humanizing experience as well as a spiritual one. There is the gradual awareness that the coming of aging for everyone is to journey once again through life in order to integrate, accept and reconcile all that has gone before. To be fully in the present and know that we have earned our experiences redeems getting older as our badge of fruitfulness. This fruitfulness is what we give back to the world. In the divine cycle of life, this fruitfulness paradoxically keeps us young!

The Coming of Aging: Learning to Live from the Inside Out is an adventure book, an intensely personal journey inviting readers to partake and share not only in the writer's journey, but in their own. It is not about how to avoid the effects of aging by changing our externals, but rather to acknowledge the wondrous mystical intuitive voice of the sacred that resides in all of us, and is imminently available and practical if we dare to trust.

Throughout the book I use a variety of names and descriptions for the *sacred*. I refer to God most frequently because that was the name I grew up with and is internalized in my psyche. As my personal relationship with the sacred deepened I struggled to become more definitive in my descriptions of those experiences and to name the very real *other*. This is not meant to replace anyone's perception of the divine. It is merely one more reflection on my personal *coming of aging* process.

I am deeply grateful for all the people in this book who danced on my path, for their stories and for sharing their lives with me. There were so many sacred moments from the sublime to the hilariously ridiculous, from sunrises on the eastern sea to the sunsets in the desert and the western ocean. I remember, too, all the mouth watering dinners campers invited me to share. I can still taste the oysters and shrimp from the Low Country. Nor can I ever forget the homey fragrance of biscuits with field peas and ham, or fried chicken and pecan pie. I gorged on Tex-Mex in the Southwest and gazillians of family favorites wherever I landed. Thank you, thank you. You are not forgotten.

I am also grateful to those who encouraged me to continue writing this book. How many times did you hold my feet to the fire or wrist to the keyboard? I give thanks to my daughter Darrah Bryans and to Lin Schreiber, the greatest Life Coach around. And thanks to my supportive writing group the MDB's for their feedback and suggestions: Christine Flaherty, Jody Hetherington and Lee Heffner.

Finally, I am filled to overflowing with gratitude to the Holy Spirit, the Inner Voice, for being my abiding presence in the great dance of life.

Jean Shula

Book I

Practicing for a New Life's Journey

Chapter 1
Toes and Water

*I live in the cross currents of the ocean: just as a rhythm seems
to be in place, the wind freshens then quickens, picks up and
tosses a wave in the opposite or sidewise direction and I am
caught in the cross currents. I feel the pull of the sea, those tugs
and pulls from underneath, the undertow, threatening and
overwhelming. When I go with it, am not afraid, the incoming
wave carries me safely to the shore and deposits me in a new
place.*
  Journal: Hatteras Island, N.C., October

If I have learned one thing as I grow older, it is that whenever angst
raises its snaky little head in the deep places of my soul, I know that I
am in for a ride on the winds of change and possible transformation.
When I was younger, I circumvented those restless feelings. Change
meant starting another diet, joining a gym, or cutting my hair. It meant
joining a book discussion group, planning something fun for the family
or switching from *Bon Appetit to Gourmet*. Knowing change is
inevitable and welcoming it, however, are two different virtues. No
matter how many times the cycle spins out, I have yet to welcome in
advance the knowledge that something new in me is about to be born.
Experience has taught me that such knowledge usually presages
unknown trips into the dark night of my own soul where struggle and
pain are not uncommon. It is one of the holy mysteries why this is so;

for the end result when I journey into the places of divine direction is ultimately a new awakening to joy. You would think by the time I was fifty I would have learned to embrace blowing out the cobwebs in my soul with song and dance!

The house held that eerily oppressive silence that only empty houses can, intensified by the deepening shadows of a cold January afternoon too quickly sliding into twilight. There were no voices, no children's laughter and teasing. There were no sibling arguments or a spouse's hollering from the nether regions. No doors slammed or upper decibel music blasted into the purple silence. On that cold day, the supposed beginning of a new year, there was no one requiring anything from me in the empty nest I currently called home. There was only dead silence and my own resentment toward the weary unending chore of paying bills and updating my calendar for the coming year. I remember thinking with a twinge of humor that not too many years ago I would have sold my soul for this kind of peace and quiet, where the hours stretched out ahead to be filled with whatever I chose. What is it, in the divine plan, that insists that we always be yearning for what we do not have? Once I yearned for silence; now that I have silence, I yearned for—what?

Yearn is a remarkably definitive word meaning so much more than simple wanting or desiring. The dictionary says that it means to be *filled* with longing or desire, understanding and sympathy. Yearn is a soul-word that expresses the longing of the heart and the psyche toward that which is ineffable. It is soulspeak, I believe, for our stretching out of the realm of ego toward the enrichment and enhancement of the person each of us is designed to be.

We do not consciously break out of the bonds of our status quo until we experience an internal shift from which we can no longer hide. In the twilight of a year just past and a new one being born, I felt the yearning for something I could not name. The heavy oppressive silence of my empty house mirrored the silence of my empty soul, and the sitting and waiting was the beginning of cracking open the secrets of my soul's yearning. I wanted back what I heard and experienced when I was three years old.

"Feed my sheep," the young man said to me as he beckoned me to come to him. He was standing in front of the pulpit from which my father was preaching that Sunday morning fifty years ago. I was prevented from running to the shepherd by the sibilant shushing of the Suffering Servant assigned to sit with me during the service. Again the young shepherd motioned me forward with a smile and the same words, "Feed my sheep." Again the SS grabbed my dress and held on while I loudly protested, "I just want to feed the sheep!"

From the choir, mother gave me her most scarifying glower and shook her head. The third time, the SS was ready. She held me fast with her fingers over my mouth. When I tried to explain after church to any and all who would listen that I saw a shepherd and I saw sheep, I was smiled at, patted and dismissed, with my father's blandishment, "She has an overactive imagination."

How sad, I thought fifty years later. That little girl heard the voice of the Divine and learned three things: 1) *imagination is suspect*; 2) *individual experience may not be respected or validated by important persons if it is out of the norm*; and 3) *hearing the "voice" of God can create conflict.* So I forgot this experience, shoved it away into the unconscious for a long time.

Yet, I thought, *there was a fourth learning, wasn't there? The voice of God was there for me at three, giving me direction, calling me into relationship with the sacred in setting the course for my life. "Feed my sheep" has been a guiding principle in governing the choices I made all my life even when totally unaware that was what I was doing.*

On that January day, the thought of feeding any more of anything to anyone was enough to make me weep. Preparing for the time when my three children would be grown, I took a degree in psychology and established a satisfying private practice with a sub-specialty in grief and bereavement. Another woman and I co-founded the local hospice. She did the nursing-medical component while I trained and supported the volunteers. When the children left home for college and my husband's days were filled as a physician, I had more time to deepen my own professional life. It was the natural order of things, I believed, part of growing older. Entering my fifth decade, I had enthusiasm and expectant energy for the next stage of our lives.

When my husband left to "date other women," the world I knew and trusted collapsed. There was no preparation, even being a therapist, for the kind of pain that accompanied the devastation and loss of husband, marriage, home, and identity. It took every second of the three years since the final divorce decree to gain back my equilibrium.

Life was beginning to settle into a new normal. I had a new house and my relationships with my children were close and warm. I was paying my bills, even dating occasionally. What was up with my psyche that I was sitting like a lump, feeling bereft and empty? Life was so full there were not enough hours to meet the needs of clients and hospice families, bereavement and AIDS support groups. Added to all of this were the requests for in-service training, plus the thousand and two details that came with this world. I might not have figured out what "feed my sheep" meant, but by God, now that I was alone and had the time, I was working on it.

Eyeing the stack of bills awaiting payment, I had a searing thought. *Everything is different but nothing has changed. Nothing has changed because you are still living just as you lived before the divorce. You are doing the same activities while you work to support a mortgage and try to gain financially. The rest of the time you're anticipating seeing the kids and looking forward to looking forward.* Maybe this was not enough. Immediately consumed by guilt, I thanked God and all the Holy Angels for my joys and blessings. The prayer did not work; it did not distract me from the bone deep weariness and knowing that I was not living a fulfilled life.

The words of a Wordsworth poem floated into my head.

The world is too much with us; late and soon
Getting and spending, we lay waste our powers:
Little we see in Nature that is ours;
We have given our hearts away, a sordid boon![1]

Was this, then, the source of my emptiness, my angst? So focused on what I was doing that my powers were not developing? Was I so distanced from the natural world, so busy doing good works, so focused on financial security that I was giving my heart away? If so, then it all was truly a sordid boon. And, oh yes, incidentally, what was my heart's desire?

Fulfillment for a woman is often tied to her relationship with a man. Was I just dragging because there was no man in my life with whom I wanted to share time and space? Was this the cost of being alone? I knew I wasn't ready to trust the intimacies of body, mind and spirit; I was yet too injured to make a healthy choice. I was still barely able to navigate the uncharted territory of living not just as a single woman, but also as a person who freely embraces the opportunity to develop her own uniqueness. I needed to learn how to take care of myself, to heal, to become whole before I had anything to offer a partner. I was paying the bills that were my obligation and responsibility; but what was the cost of this way of living in terms of becoming whole?

The shadows lengthened in the room. I switched on the light. "What," I wondered out loud, "can I do to *change* and become *whole?*" How could I turn on the light in my own soul, lighten up, become enlightened? I sat up straighter in my chair. Just the thought caught my attention. Thoughts came fast from a source not yet explored. *Your whole way of doing things is a reaction to the external world. Nothing external can create the change for which you yearn. Learn to live from the inside-out not the outside-in.*

And so the epiphany of that January began to sing in my soul. It began to glow in the dark of my home and my heart. I felt younger, fresher, than I had in years. *Inside-out, inside -out, inside-out* echoed in the hollowness of my head like a mantra gaining power on the breath. Writing about it now, these words still have the power to infuse my being with joyful exuberance and set my fingers tingling. I remember so well the accompanying feelings of anticipatory wonder and expectation. Something in me was about to be changed. For the

15

moment all thoughts of worry about what this journey might mean in terms of reaching into my own inner darkness were forgotten. I just sat and basked in the quiet euphoria that is like sharing a joke with God.

I wanted more. I lifted up my voice and said, "Yes! I want more of this. I want to live with this energy I'm feeling, whatever it is. I want to live in such a way that I can share this joy and well-being with everyone. I want to experience this all the time. I want to live *from the inside-out!*" In that moment, all I wanted was to remain in that transcendent state forever. I felt euphoric. I laughed with joy and the tears that I rarely shed came freely.

Not willing to give up on the moment, but desperately willing to follow this wave wherever it took me, I gleefully opened up my imagination, my *over-active imagination,* to the possibilities of living from the inside-out. What would I have to change in order to experience life in this way?

Change your life, take some time off. Clearly I felt overloaded and dried out. *Three weeks,* I thought. *I could take three weeks off, get quiet, breathe deeply, renew.* The euphoria started to slip. Okay, maybe three weeks wouldn't be enough. *Six weeks. Six whole weeks to sit in the sun and read books. I could write. I could sleep and pray.* My soul was weeping with the wonder of such a thought, yet the joy began to fade.

"What?" I asked the room. "What's wrong with taking six weeks?" Something wasn't connecting; I wasn't getting it. I grabbed the chair, closed my eyes and aimed in a direction I had never dared before. "I will take a year off and call it a sabbatical!" The bubble inside began to rise again. My mind sped in all directions accepting and rejecting dozens of impractical schemes from selling t-shirts on a beach in Bali to renting a cottage by the sea in Ireland.

Finally, I began to affirm, out loud, that I would take a leap of faith: "I will take a significant leave of absence." I sat in my own upper room, wrapped in impossible joy and made a conscious decision to leave this place for a trip into the unknown for one whole year because, as improbable as it sounded, there was a voice *inside* urging me on. The confirmation, or maybe recognition, of this voice established a level of lightness in my psyche that was a wholly new experience. At the time,

I did not know it, but I was getting my first lesson in living from the inside out. It was necessary for me to stop all the mind-chatter spelling out those practical reasons why taking time off at this juncture was impractical, impossible, and incomprehensible, and simply affirm that there was another way to live. Figuring that out was the next step.

Right in front of me was the unholy trinity that governed my life: checkbook, calendar, and appointment book. There was a moment of hesitation and questioning when I realized how many requests I had for speaking around the country in the coming year. This was the kind of success I thought I wanted. I could get paid to travel and to speak, both of which I love. There were clients depending on me. What opportunities was I throwing away? Now that the decision to take time off was made, the how's and when's demanded attention. As ludicrous as it sounds, within fifteen minutes I knew what I had to do and how I would do it.

I totaled up everything I owed, except the mortgage on my house. If I lived very strictly on a budget, I could put every cent I made into paying off educational loans and set money aside for the trip. If I worked very diligently, I would be able to pay off everything and leave for my sabbatical in nine months. If I rented my house furnished, it would cover the mortgage and maintenance. Finally, from childhood vacation experiences, I knew I could live cheaper on the road than I could at home if I camped. And I could buy a used camper if I sold my car.

I went to bed with this grand scheme spinning in my head. Still giggling softly, full of holy glee and joyous expectation, I placed my hands on my stomach and thought of new life and birth, at my age!

Chapter 2
Gestation

Standing on the curb in the shivery half-light of a January dawn, I lifted my head and breathed in the tangy salt air scents of a Massachusetts fishing town. To my left the river that ran to meet the sea was misty murky beyond the pilings where a few die-hard vessels circled as tidal forces beyond their control twirled them at their moorings. To my right, the familiarity of the neighborhood weighed in with a few brave lights glowing in steamy upstairs bathroom windows and softly lit downstairs kitchens. The smells of coffee and toast and oatmeal with maple sugar lay in that direction, warm and homey, closed in with all that is comforting. I turned and stared straight ahead.

Not yet quite light nor yet still dark, the dawn felt less like a promise of sunrise than a threat of a colder bleaker day to come. It was a time for serious ruminations, for honest evaluation of the tossing and turnings of the night just past, for wondering if all the decisions of yesterday were merely the workings of a manic moment when anything seemed possible; or if they were the inspirations of divine creativity. Somehow it seemed to be a pregnant moment, this stepping off the curb which I had done hundreds of times without thought or care to start my day with a brisk walk through town. Yet something hugey powerful seemed to be holding me to the spot. *What?* I cried out inside.

Pretending that all was usual, I bent and twisted at the waist, stretching muscles, all the while testing the words of the promise I made the day before. *I will take time off. I will take time to think and reflect about living from the inside out.* The same frisson of excitement passed through me, the same lightening of the load that I felt the day before. Checking whether or not the neighbors had begun to notice that I was not moving from my curbside position, I said the magic word out loud just to test my reaction. "Sabbatical!" I hissed, anticipating the surge of energy that suffused all the way to my fingertips.

Understanding dawned. The idea I so madly tossed out into the ether the night before, to camp across the country with no agenda and no schedule for a year, was simply the vehicle for something far more profound. The purpose of my life was not to go camping; it was to LISTEN to the voice within. It was to TRUST what I hear. It was to ACT out of that listening trust. I blinked my eyes, standing completely still. I felt that time had raced ahead of me and I had been rooted curbside for hours. My watch said five minutes. How could my whole life take on such enormous shift and insight in only five minutes? Surely there should be a dove descending, or a voice from heaven proclaiming "She's starting to get it! Hallelujah!"

I stood in the frozen early morning, exhilarated and humbled, scared and defenseless, straining for guidance and direction. Listen. Trust. Act. Strip away the trappings of religiosity down to the bed rock tenets of faith without equivocation; I-Thou in its purest sense. Learning to live from the inside out means a minute by minute dependence on the belief that "the kingdom of God is within" me, you, the guy down the street. Most of all, my racing mind proclaimed, the voice of the divine, of the energy that makes my river roar and neighborhood awaken, is *available.* If I choose to believe that, then I dare the next step and say *it is available to me.*

Out of the mists of the morn came the mystical teaching from some primal source that this knowledge of dependence on the divine is the grounding and connectedness that will sustain me through my journey into the unknown. I stepped off the curb to begin my walk, having no precognition that what I started this day would literally save my life on several levels many times in the coming year.

Over and over people ask me to describe what the voice inside sounds like.

—Is it a real voice?

—Is it separate from my own internal voice?

—How do I know I can trust such airy-fairy schmoozle?

—Why doesn't God speak to everyone?

—How can I (the asker) learn to do this?

My profound enlightened response is: I don't know. All I know is that my memory and journal of that morning are like a giant canvas on which was painted a scene that has color, texture and meaning, like a great work of art. Like great art this canvas has the power to reach out and grab all my senses. My response was a deep internal shift in the core of my being.

One of the major insights of that shift was that I must practice what I was learning. The practicing was a tacit understanding that I was making a choice to change the pattern of my behavior and my conscious acceptance of the reality of the Divine. The mechanics of that choice and how it works are easier to explain than trying to dissect a mystical experience which taught me to listen to the voice of God whispering in my soul. Standing on that curb in front of my house I had reached a finite point where I knew I had to either put up or shut up.

God-talk was part of my life. I grew up with it, studied it, practiced it, analyzed it, and yakked it to death. Curbside, I realized that talk really is cheap. It has it uses, but sometimes in the face of our most poignant and meaningful moments both sacred and horrorific, *there are no words.* There is only experience and belief; feeling and perception. Standing there contemplating what it meant to hand myself over to God in a literal sense, I had no words.

This was not about a liturgical exercise, formal or intercessory prayer, doing it the right way, or being theologically correct or scripturally sound. It came down to a very simple concept: the Divine is either available or not; which way do I choose to live? I made a choice based partly on previous experience, somewhat on perception, a little bit of intuition, a small dose of agnosticism and the rest intellectual. I was gearing up to take the famous Kierkegaardian "leap in the dark toward the light."

This leap meant that God-talk was to be replaced by God-listening. Over the course of the months of trip preparation, if I were very blessed, I would hear God-talking. I was in the on-going process of being born again. The time had come to make choices about whom or what governed my life and my decisions, and to recognize that I needed to learn how to depend totally on the spiritual for my wholeness and my safety. Need I mention that some trepidation also came along for the ride?

This sounds more dramatic than the reality. The shifts taking place were quiet and deep. Despite my efforts to describe what I was experiencing, I did not, like many saints and sacred figures of various religions, dance on the altar or strip down to nakedness and sing for joy. Intrinsically, I knew that if I were going to be able to go alone into the world without fear or paranoia, I would first have to learn *how* to listen, *how* to trust and *how* to act.

There is good precedence for taking some time to allow new revelations to sink into the psyche. Jesus of Nazareth took forty days. Saul of Tarsus took three years. Buddha took six years of extreme ascetic living. And Mohammed took five years of annual solitary retreats. I am a woman. I had exactly nine months.

Listening: "Be still and know that I am God"[2]
My morning walk was an excellent way to begin. In the quiet of the early dawn before the tangle of daily commitments intruded, before the town was alive with exhaust fumes and frenetic purpose, and before I became the receptacle for my psychotherapy clients' hurts and pains, the stillness of the world became a sacred grove in which to infuse the body, clear the mind, and quiet the soul. This was the time for meditative or prayerful walking; a time to shut out mundane thoughts and sink into the silence within. What a natural way to practice listening.

Unlike walking for purely physical activity, meditative walking is not focused on the amount of time, distance or pace. Rather, it combines all the healthy physical elements with stress reduction and emotional/spiritual well-being. Perhaps more importantly, walking with meditative purpose taught me how to quiet the turmoil of my over-stimulated mind by stilling the mind-chatter, that relentless internal litany of garbled words that tumble through my waking moments. At any given moment my mind can distract me with a yakkity cyclical list of concerns from toenails to world peace.

Unfortunately, my prayer life frequently was an extension of all this chatter. I merely transferred my attention to the Creator and continued to expel the words. What I was on the cusp of learning at dawn that day was the significance of silence.

If I was going to accept the availability of the Divine in a meaningful and purposeful way in my innermost being, I had to prepare the way for the voice to be heard. The words of the psalm became instantly relevant and significant. "Be still and know that I am God." What a wealth of understanding comes with that phrase. I am not in charge of the universe. Imagine that!

All the mind-chatter is an endless attempt to bring control into a life and situations that ultimately seem to be without it; it is an attempt to bring order out of chaos. Yet here were the ancient words reminding me that I could let go of it all and simply be still and allow the Orderer of Order, the Planner of Divine Plans, the Artist of the Grand Mosaic be in charge. What a relief! The universe would not fall apart if I missed a detail about anything and everything in my purview.

The Psalm seemed to be speaking to me. "Be still and *know* that I am who you need me to be, and your part will become clearer." And part of what I was learning was that I needed a clear and unambiguous pipeline to the very Source of what was keeping the stars in their heavens and the earth spinning on its axis. I needed to learn how to rely on that deep internal Spirit to guide and to be in charge. Stepping off the curb became a daily ritual in Practicing the Presence.

After a few weeks, the rhythm of practicing listening became richer, deeper and automatic. This is the form that emerged.

—I began the walk by standing still, breathing deeply and acknowledging the presence of the Creator in the innermost place of body, mind and spirit. *"Be still and know that I am God."*

—I asked for direction with a simple prayer. *"I will not move from this place until you tell me which way to go."*

—I waited for the inner *nudge.* For me this was usually more of a positive knowing, a nudge of intuition, than hearing a dramatic voice. (Each person is unique, so I assume this part of the process is also unique.)

—As I walked, I concentrated on breathing deeply, finding the rhythm that was most comfortable. It was helpful to visualize light and wholeness coming into my body with each breath. It helped to stop the mind-chatter by staying centered in the present moment.

—When mind-chatter intruded, I simply acknowledged it and gently pushed it away by going back to either concentrating on my breathing or by repeating the words of the psalm like a mantra. *"Be still and know that I am God."*

—At each street or crossroad I asked the question, "Which way?" and waited for the nudge.

As I became more comfortable, I began to use the natural world as part of my recognition of *hearing* the Divine. I listened for the voice in the wind off the water, in the voices of children as they walked to school, in the opening of buds on the trees and the flowers in the yards I passed.

I practiced walking in this manner almost every day for nine months. Did my attention and belief every waver? Yes and Yes. There were days when I thought that if I ever told anyone what I was doing they would cart me away. I would remind myself that as a psychotherapist I would have a difficult time explaining that I was developing an inner ear that listened for the voice of the Creator. There was no question, however, that the benefits from my new attitude and structure each morning were enormous in terms of peace of mind and faith. But I would be less than honest if I did not admit that normal doubts were part of my new chatter. One day stands out particularly in my memory.

I was walking downtown near the waterfront park in the spring on a beautiful clear morning. It was one of those New England days when the sky was so blue your back teeth hurt; and the sun sparkled on the water like lively 4th of July fireworks. It was one of those rare and perfect days that tempt you to stay out in it as long as possible. When it was time to turn toward home I came to the street and automatically asked which way. While waiting for the answer, I realized that I really didn't want to ask for direction because I had a strong desire to walk home via the water route and not the town route.

I stood there alone on the curb and laughed at the ridiculous fluffhead I was becoming. *What makes you think God gives one little care which way you go home?* I derided myself. *Right or left. What difference does it make in the scheme of things? You have sold yourself one huge load of ca-ca and all of this is the proverbial sound and fury signifying nothing! What in heavens name do you think you're doing? This is a stupid exercise! It just isn't important whether or not you go right or left!*

In that moment, for the first time in my life, I heard a voice in my mind that was distinctly not mine. "This is not about going right or left; it is about listening. There will be times when my voice is all you will have, the only voice you will hear."

I cannot remember which route I walked home that day, but I will never forget the reality of that experience. When the truth is made plain, it sinks in the soul with a rightness than cannot be denied. This truth kept me going for the remaining six months of my gestation.

Trust: "Look around. What do you see?"

Trust is huge; it is tricky and difficult on so many levels. Just saying the word is sometimes enough to set up every doubt, every fear and every uncertainty in the human condition.

We come into the world absolutely dependent on the skills of others for our survival. In psychology there is the term "good enough." A mother or caregiver only has to be "good enough" for us to thrive physically and emotionally. This is the beginning of trust, without which we are in danger of the failure to thrive. So in a very real sense, learning to trust is the first and foremost task of becoming a whole person.

The paradox is that while we are infants and leaning on the goodwill of others, we are also learning that not every person is there for us 100%

of the time. We are learning that when others are not trustworthy or let us down, we can begin to do certain things for ourselves. In a sense, the breaking of trust is the beginning of the necessary lessons that will enable us to become healthy individuals capable of taking care of ourselves and others.

Therefore, having a good-enough parent means that we had the basic necessities, that there was enough trust for us to survive and to be able to grow. It also means that caregivers are off the hook of perfection, that unattainable goal in which every need, every want and desire is met without reservation; that we never had to cry for a feeding, a hug, comfort, fever or temper. All needs were anticipated and met. What parent/person could possibly meet this criterion? The answer is, no one can. In fact, this kind of anticipatory unconditional love is part of the description of the Divine; it is part of what makes God, God.

I clearly remember my feelings of frustration and inadequacy when my first child woke up crying from each nap. I was always there in an instant, but it was never quick enough to prevent his crying, and that tore at my heart. "Why don't you trust me?" I asked him. "I always come to you and feed you. I change your diaper. Don't you know by now that I am here for you? Have I ever let you down?"

Ah, but the point was, that poor little guy had no way of making his own personal wishes known. He had no other means of connecting, or recourse to survival but to remind me that he was here and hungry now! *And mom, if I cry, will you come just one more time?* He was learning the basic code of trust, over and over and over again. He had an imperfect mother who sometimes slept through the first outcry, or was too tired to move immediately. Sometimes I was just praying that this time his cry was a sleep-induced noise and slumber would reclaim him. Over time, he learned that he could trust me for his basics, but not always on his schedule.

Over time, all of us learn that trust is a precious commodity. As we step out into the world, part of our maturation process is learning whom to trust and whom not to. Not everyone is as trustworthy as mom and dad; not everyone has our best interests at heart. We are all too familiar with the horrors of moms and dads who abuse their children from the start. These are the little ones who sadly learn that the world is a hostile and terrifying place where trust is buried so far underground that it lies in the catacombs and tunnels of human consciousness. The children of all ages whose lives are interrupted by war, famine, pestilence and the indifference of affluence will spend the rest of their lives suspicious of trusting anyone or any policy or any promise. There are adults who experience betrayal and misery at the hands of people and institutions they thought they could trust. This threatens their lives at the most basic level by knocking out the underpinnings upon which they built their expectations and futures.

"Trust me," says the snake oil salesman. "Trust me," says the pedophile. "Trust me," says the political candidate, the president, and the senator. "Trust me," says the real estate salesman, the investment counselor, the stockbroker, the CEO. "Trust me," says the priest, the psychiatrist, the doctor, the lawyer. "Trust me," cracks the comedian on Saturday Night Live, and we all laugh. "Yeah, right. And aren't we the fools if we do."

In our popular culture where we are guided by the commandments of the bottom-line, and genuflect before the altar of celebrity reverence, *trust* has become at best a word that gets a snicker, and at worst is a pejorative term. It has become a word that glides most frequently from the mouths of those who least represent the values we have an intrinsic desire to believe in. In some sense, contemporary life is a series of lessons in discovering that trust is undesirable when it is linked to naiveté. Unfortunately, when we experience the world as untrustworthy, usually through a series of hurtful events and people in which we have misplaced our trust, we become stunted by the greatest loss of all, *mistrust in ourselves*. We no longer believe that we have the discernment necessary to know where and in whom to place our trust.

Fortunately, trust is inextricably bound up with faith and belief. It is arguably difficult to have faith without trust, and trust without faith of some kind. And for most of us, our belief system informs how we express or practice them. Our faith-belief is part of our identity whether we practice or not. It informs others and ourselves about who we are and with whom we share our belonging. I am an American-German-Scots-Irish protestant woman. I am an African-American-Baptist man. I am a Swiss-American-Lebanese-Shiite woman. I am an American-Italian-Catholic.

Trust, therefore, becomes one of the ways and means we have of identifying with a larger group. You guys "out there" may be out to better yourselves at my expense, but you guys "in here," in my group, you are trustworthy. We have a shared sense of belonging that I can trust—most of the time. And I can trust that whether or not I have had any experience of the trustworthy God, I can rely on the group's trust. If you guys say it is so, then I can go along. My experience may tell me that putting trust in something as nebulous as Spirit, or Creator, or God does not work, but the group has a history of events and collections of stories that are deeper, wider and more powerful than anything I can think up. So ok, I trust what the group says. And my group says that I can trust God, so I say I can, too.

What confronted me on my daily walks was that I had reached a point where I was internalizing my trust in the Creator; it was no longer enough for it to be a part of my identification with a larger group. It was becoming intensely personal. *How do I know that God keeps promises?* I asked myself. *Look around you. What do you see?* responded the voice inside. As I walked, it occurred to me that I was like a baby crying out when my immediate *hunger* pains for absolute knowing were seemingly ignored in the immediacy of now. This thrust me back on the basic fundamentals of using all my senses to stay in the present.

I am in the here and now. I see the sky is blue and the trees are lacey against the sky. The sun shimmers off the water, and all around me I hear the sounds of life in the thrumming of people and cars. I feel the warmth of the breeze stirring my hair where it tickles the back of my neck. And what earthy smells drift over the mown grass carrying just a hint of flowers at the peak of their perfume.

What can you trust about all of this? Looking around I was mystified at first. What had this to do with trusting? The more I puzzled, the deeper into the question I fell. What could I trust about this world? What is so fundamental, so basic that I take it for granted and never think about it as a significant promise of the trustworthiness of Creation? I looked around me, and what did I see? The earth, the sky, the sun. *An excellent place to start with trust*, the voice said.

No matter what happens on any given day, wonderful or horrible, the one thing I could count on was that the night will be over, the daylight will appear; the sun will rise even on a rainy day. The earth spins on her axis while the stars stay in their heavens. The moon and the tides will stay their courses, and objects fall down not up. Winter always blossoms into spring, and summer harvests into fall. Each day and season is part of the eternal truth. I can trust that this is so. From there I began to see with fresh eyes the nature of goodness all around me. I started to look for the face of God in strangers. I began noticing the unselfish acts of neighbors and friends. I became more attuned to recognizing the verbal and nonverbal cues of people who dedicated themselves to lightening the burdens of others in body, mind and spirit. I saw it all around me and I knew that I could trust that the Divine presence is everywhere. Trust is a choice of attitude, an affirmation of the constancy and reliability of God.

Practicing this trust every day while walking, opened huge great vistas in my interior life. But I must confess that as I was growing increasingly aware of the myriad ways God's trustworthiness is manifest in the world, I could also be swamped by old feelings of betrayal and hurt. Sometimes when I read the paper or listened to the news, I wondered how on earth any of us could trust that all would be well. Trust can be a fragile thing when overwhelmed by personal and collective woes. On those days, both then and now, I have to return to the question: *What do you see?* I start at the basic level once again. What is the absolute rock bottom that I can identify to rely on and trust? The sheer simplicity of this daily reminder holds eternal truths. I see the sun coming over the horizon to start a new day and it is enough. It is a beginning.

Every morning I walked into the trusting place where I drew deep peace into my soul and committed one more time to quiet the mind-chatter, to listen to the voice of God, and to trust what I heard. Every day for all the months I prepared to travel, I carried a wondrous anticipation that something was growing in me that was taking on a life of its own. Trying to figure out what that was led me into the third phase.

Act: "Faith without works is dead."[3]

Stepping off the curb and turning right or left is an *act* of faith and trust. Without the action, the belief is stillborn. I could come home from a meditative walk and know that I experienced the nudge of the Divine and trust in its authenticity; but without becoming actively involved in the process I would be living only half a life.

One of things that I had already learned in my journey of faith was the duality of God's purpose. Insights and deeper knowledge are not for the sole purpose of making me or anyone else a better, kinder, wiser, healthier, wealthier person. As attractive an idea as this is, as desirable from the standpoint of individual growth and happiness this seems, this is a stunted, ego-centric view of the hugeness of God's purpose and love.

The other side of the equation is that each person's gifts of consciousness and actions are for the building up of the collective, the whole community. Our gifts are not only for ourselves, but for the betterment of the conditions of others. It is our *response* to the listening and trusting which becomes our *responsibility*. In every major religion there are clear imperatives to feed the hungry, clothe the naked, take care of widows and orphans, and give comfort to the sick and dying. Our actions are the extension of the inner flow of continual communication with and trusting in the power of the Divine Spirit.

It was late June and I quietly left my house before 6AM, hoping, *needing*, to start my walk before the town awoke and was inundated by tourists who interfered annoyingly with my holy time. It was difficult to listen to the Voice when my senses were bombarded with the cacophony of increased summer traffic. Tourists streamed to the docks where parents were yelling at their kids and kids were yelling just for the fun of it. My soul longed for peace and quiet to work out some knotty details of my new divine life.

I slipped to the front curb and began my ritual: pray, breathe, ask, wait, trust, and go. Suddenly, the utter futility of what I was doing swept over me and left me stunned. Where did this come from? Self-doubt raised its syrupy little voice, slurping into my meditative quietness with a vengeance, proclaiming that I was never going to pull off this fantasy trip for a whole year. What had I really done to prepare except pay off some financial obligations and learn new meditative techniques? Both of which were beneficial in the present and would make life easier in the future. The threatening loss of the dream dropped into my psyche like stones in a paddle wheel, slowing down the momentum and gumming up the works.

Bereft, I wandered down to the river avoiding the early morning fishermen and families going off for the day. I barely had the heart to ask, "Right or left?" Somehow I ended up farther away than usual, behind the old deserted Towle Silver factory, sitting on an outcropping of rock, staring at the Merrimac River. This tidal river with the sun dancing on the peaks of the currents, this river at once treacherous and welcoming, powerful and yielding, curled like a ribbon on the green fields of a hundred New England towns. A seemingly unrelated question popped into my head: *How do you get on the river?* Since getting on the river was not a viable activity at the moment, I dismissed it as evidence of my wandering thoughts. It persisted, however, until I sat up and began to take notice.

Given my deep involvement in the mystical process of learning the language of God over the past six months, I was thrilled to feel the familiar stirrings of the internal shift I call the *voice*. The tidal river before me was wide, deep and tricky to navigate. Standing on the bank, I heard its voice in the rushing swiftness of the incoming tide. In that moment, I experienced a renewed respect for the beauty of its powerful potential. But I could not *know* the river until I became a part of it, which was a possibility only if I chose to either jump in and swim or launch a boat and ride it out.

For six months I had been sitting on the banks of my trip. The time had come for me to jump off the pier and immerse myself in the river of my life. It was time for me to actively make plans for telling my family and friends that I would no longer be available in the same old way after September first.

Suddenly my head was abuzz with all the chores before me. First and foremost, my clients deserved to know that I was not abandoning them and that we had three months to say goodbye and to find other resources for them as needed. It was time to risk telling my story to my loved ones and trust that they would encourage me on my way. The thousands of details that needed attention were staggering. Rent my house; sell my car; buy a camper. Mysteriously, none of this felt overwhelming. It all felt right, and very simple. The time had come to honor my internal messages by taking care of the externals of my life.

Walking home that day I realized that I was no longer annoyed by the honking, bustling summer sounds of a portside town. As soul stretching as the months of meditative walking had been, as serenely grounding and awe-inspiring they had appeared, they were yet only the beginning of something more to come. Skimming home that day I was aware of the people, places and sounds in a way that was new and refreshing. Far from coming to the end of my learning, I was at the jumping off point to the unknown. All I had to do was be open to what was next.

Standing on the curb in the misty light of a summer dawn, I looked at the river to my left and was amazed at the beautiful mist riding on the water like clouds kissing the tops of mountains. To my right the neighborhood awakened with the familiar smells of coffee and bacon and the symphonic sounds of doors slamming, and people calling out their goodbyes and be carefulls. *Right or left?* I automatically asked. And the answer was new. *Straight down the middle.*

Chapter 3
Going with the Flow

*Nine months to detach, deregulate and probably decompensate!
I surely couldn't have entertained even the thought of this whole
project if I weren't ready in some deep place inside. It has taken
me this long to detach from material possessions—those things
I needed to have around me when my world fell apart.*
Journal: Newburyport, MA, January

The discipline of walking and meditating had begun to give me a
structure that soon became as necessary to me as food, for it was indeed
feeding me on several levels. My body was toning and getting fit for
endurance. My mind was channeling into quiet waters away from
chaotic chatter, and my spirit was opening up to the unlimited
possibilities of being free in my inner self.

This was scary territory for a middle-aged woman whose whole life
thus far had been proscribed by the rules of good conduct and right
associations. From student to wife, and mother, I had done everything
right on schedule. The things I did for myself, like going to graduate
school in my forties, were always done within the confines of whatever
time was left over from my *real* commitments. So here I was, suddenly
thrust into freedom for the first time in my life and I had no idea how
to proceed, except to cling to the old and familiar even if the cost was
stunting my soul.

Something seminal, however, was taking place; I was coming back
to life and to the recognition of my own regressive behavior in the midst

of pain and overwhelming grief and sorrow. Like most souls when wounded, I had regressed to a place of remembered safety by duplicating the only life I had known. I was unconsciously desperate to duplicate security and happiness.

How consuming it had become to keep all the tangible mementos of my marriage and family life! My new house was full of the furniture and memorabilia from twenty-eight years of marriage and family life. In my single state all those things assumed a significance that they had never before exercised. Even my schedule was based on the rhythms of our family life; breakfast, lunch and dinner at regular proscribed times. Even bath and bed times were committed to a relinquished pattern no longer necessary when there was one person instead of five to accommodate.

In some primal way all of these possessions and forms gave me the illusion of stability, security and most of all, belonging. I had become the keeper of a flame in a deserted temple. It took an act of Nature to rock my entrenchment.

An early blizzard the previous winter blanketed our lovely coastal town in piles of white fluff, closing streets, schools, and traffic. A huge wonderful giddiness gripped the community. Commuters could not get to Boston, teachers and students had an unexpected holiday while little ones made snow angels with their parents. Sleds, cross-country skis, and toboggans miraculously appeared in the streets. The watering holes usually packed by tourists quickly filled with cheerful neighbors escaping the claustrophobic feeling New Englanders call cabin fever. Freedom reigned!

My great friend, Christine, walked to my place and like everyone else, we threw off our work shackles and went out to play. As the day progressed, we added other friends to our impromptu roving party, going from one restaurant to another listening to music, arguing politics, and in general living out the dictum to "eat, drink and be merry." Despite the merriment and bonhomie, at six o'clock I became restless and uncomfortable. It was time to go home. It was not that I was bored or socially depleted; quite the contrary. I was having a wonderful time chatting and laughing. As I began to gather up my gear, people started asking me where I was going, why was I leaving? I remember feeling empty and disoriented. Six o'clock was the anchor time for all good families to be safely home where they were settling in for dinner and the evening.

In that moment I was paralyzed by the paradoxical maelstrom my life had become. At one and the same time I felt both the devastation of being alone, and the incredible realization that I was *free* to be wherever I chose. The reality slammed into me. Six o'clock was probably still being observed in many homes, but it had become pointless to me, just one more piece of my old life that had to be cast off. I had hauled that particular anchor. If I did not want to be set adrift, I needed to find new meanings and new balances between being alone and being free.

When the words "straight down the middle" echoed in my consciousness, I knew they could not be taken literally. From my curb there was only right or left, no middle way was possible. Taken as metaphor, however, the words became significantly richer; alive with possibilities which took me into the realm of examining the nature of *balance* and *discernment*.

I had some vague notion of what balance meant; something to do with one side being equal to the other. Yet we often speak about the *balance of nature,* or something is *hanging in the balance.* Justice is portrayed as a blindfolded goddess holding *perfectly balanced* scales in her outstretched hand. *On balance*, meaning everything being equal, we make a choice between several opportunities. The world seems lopsided when there is no longer a *balance of power.* Conversely, when someone exhibits irrational behavior we say that person is *unbalanced.* Clearly then, balance is something that represents a positive force in our lives, something worth striving toward, something worth acquiring, a venerable ideal .

Teetering on the edge of the curb straining to listen to the Inner Voice, I only knew what balance was by its very lack in my life. Up to this point, there was no mandate to think about balance as anything other than a word or concept used in passing. I never realized that as busy and overwhelmed as I sometimes felt juggling all the demands on my love and attention, these very components were all about balance being built into my system.

Laughing and arguing with teenagers was a marvelous antidote to the heavy emotional baggage of psychotherapy clients. Listening to my husband's day, snuggling in bed, even doing the laundry were all dynamic and creative ways that balanced the sometimes overwhelming issues that came with the territory of my chosen life. When I had this kind of equilibrium, I didn't recognize it. It was just the way life was: the blissful state of being able to take balance for granted. If any part became overpowering, there would soon be something else to tip the scale back in another direction.

My possessions became the symbol of all the rich fulfillment of a life balanced by energetic loving relationships. My current house had become the repository for the tangible history of our family; a museum of records that we truly existed and were not a romanticized vision born of my isolation. I was so focused on keeping the externals in place that the internal journey became marginal. It was inattention that was feeding my emptiness.

Over the months of walking and concentrating on *Listen, Trust, Act,* I was preparing to wrestle with my existential loneliness, with recognizing that the old norms and forms no longer applied to me; and with this knowledge I was uncovering new meaning to my existence. I could no longer dwell in the land of Divorced Empty Nest and be whole. The journey I was embarking upon was becoming equally metaphysical as physical. Was this the balance, then?

While on my early AM walk, I passed a schoolyard playground. Countless times I had walked by that yard, but on that particular day I stopped, spellbound by the teeter-totter. In my mind's eye I saw myself and my best friend in third grade slowly balancing. We aspired to that perfect state wherein if neither of us moved too quickly, and slowly took our feet off the ground, we could, for as long as we didn't become itchy or sneeze, hold that place of perfect balance, absolutely still and immobile. "Is this the balance you mean?" I asked the Inner Voice? "This static place which stops all motion, this scarcely obtainable state where there is no breathing, no laughter, no tears?" Is this what balance is all about, two opposites so keenly tuned, so fragile, that holding it becomes an art and disruption only a breath away?

On my walks I began to wonder if this perfect state of balance is ever achievable for more than a few seconds, or if it was at all possible. I looked at the myriad diversity of nature's abundance, and knew that whenever anything upset those balances, the whole organism colludes to bring it back to *homeostasis*, a new place of equilibrium. This is what we call evolving or change. Things cannot go back to the way they were before. New life comes at the cost of this evolutionary process. Sitting perfectly still on a teeter-totter may be a challenge, but sailing fearfully high and dropping breathtakingly low are much more dynamic in seeking homeostasis. Isn't this how we learn our life's lessons? Perfect balance gives us a few seconds of needed rest, but it is the tipping into one direction or another that thrusts us back into interaction with life and ultimately into seeking our own center. This state, I realized, was similar to the one we call deep contemplation and centering, being perfectly in the middle of the road!

This rumination reminded me of what Thomas Kelly wrote in his little book *The Testament of Devotion*.[4] He said that if we practice the stillness of centering, it stays at the core of our deepest self all the while we are living and interacting with the externals of our world. This action is called *simultaneity,* the act of being perpetually connected to God in the innermost depths of our being, yet simultaneously going about our daily commitments. There is a free flow back and forth, each informing the other. I am happy I remembered this as I walked each day practicing my listening. Internalizing the Inner Voice, holding it deep in my sinews so that it is a part of every thought and action must be similar to Kelly's simultaneity. Perhaps this is closer to true balance than merely trying not to be overwhelmed by the people and responsibilities in my life.

There was so much to contemplate as I prepared myself to leave all that was familiar and venture on my own. The trip was taking shape. I would have no schedule, no itinerary, and no reservations, with three notable exceptions.

- The children and I would meet to share Christmas at Hilton Head.

- I would meet my brother in California when his teaching year was finished in June.
- And for some as yet unknown reason I would spend time at Lake of the Ozarks.

This last item was a holy mystery. Over and over in the last few months, this place, wherever it was, kept cropping up. First it was in my subconscious, then in books, and later in conversations. I had no idea why, but I knew I had to get to Lake of the Ozarks—eventually.

If I were going to be true to my promise to live from the inside out, I would have to honor the commitment all the way. Just like my daily walks, I planned to ask each day the metaphoric discernment question of right or left, and follow where the Voice lead. Already, several months before my planned departure, I knew I wanted to follow the sea down the East Coast, so my real question each day would be, do I go or stay? The pull of camping on the ocean was strong and unquestioning. I needed to be by the water, at least for the first stage of my journey. I instinctively knew I needed the water to heal.

Down by the river, I watched the tidal currents race in to the shore filling up the crannies with smooth dark water, then gradually recede leaving muddy banks exposed to the briny air. *The real balance of nature*, I think. Then I stare, mesmerized by the constant change, the motion of in and out, the ebb and flow of the tides governed by the moon. I knew what I was straining to understand about balance. Life is less about perfect opposites that keep us in check than it is about the ebb and flow of the currents in our lives.

We flow outward in a great pouring of our selves to our commitments in the world. Then, like the sea, we must ebb back toward our center seeking the source, the beginning and ending, for all our energies and dreams. Without this motion, we pour ourselves out endlessly dashing our energies against the sand which absorbs it until our sea is empty. Living from the inside, the center, getting into the ebb and flow means that we are constantly renewing until we draw our last breath. The thought of all the beaches ahead of me made me squirm with the anticipation of the discovery of renewal.

37

Chapter 4
Saying Goodbye Well

Summer is over. The time has come to leave. Today was my last walk in the early morning sunlight through the town, calling out my goodbyes to the pathways that have nurtured me for nine months. Tomorrow I leave. Oh my God! Tomorrow I leave! There's no turning back. Terminated with clients, resigned from the boards, farewell dinners with friends. My house is in good hands, the Falcon is loaded. Tonight is the worst part: I say goodbye to children and my best friends. All the years of lessons in leave-taking are deserting me now!
Journal: Newburyport, MA, September

Goodbyes are hard. They are so difficult, so genuinely uncomfortable that for most of my life I frequently abstained from saying them. I am not alone. Much of our language aids our obfuscating. "See you later." "Have a good day." *Hasta la vista, au revoire, auf wiedersehn, ciao, tata.* All of these imply that we will meet again, that we're certainly not going to get all sloppy sentimental about leave-taking or make a big deal out of it. How many times have we heard someone say, "I hate goodbyes. I never say them?" No matter what language we speak, we share the universal desire to avoid and deny the finality of saying goodbye. There's a superstitious jinx about saying the words. In my case, it is one more example of ignoring what is going on inside. I have learned the hard way how ignoring this seemingly small bit of ritual can close the heart.

By the time I was eight years old, my family had moved five times. That was five times in my formative years that I had to leave all that was familiar and safe. It didn't take me long to figure out that the best way not to hurt or be scared was not to feel. I learned not to feel by focusing on the future, not the past. By the time I was eight, however, this lesson was so internalized that allowing myself to feel any pain at anyone's leave-taking was not an option. Put down roots? Why would I want to do that when there was so much out there to explore? This particular quirk made me the ideal wife for a doctor whose training and career dictated that we live in six states including Alaska. In all of those moves I never cried once. In every photograph there I am, waving merrily, smiling hugely, excited to be *going* not *leaving.* Not one tear in sight; that is, not until Alaska.

Internalized lesson or not, something very moving happened to me during the two years we lived in Anchorage. I invested myself in the people of that community. I allowed myself to care, to befriend and be friend-ed unto. There was something mystical about the totality of our experience while we lived there. For the first time ever I felt I was living in a community of strength and compassion that was filled with authenticity and love. Call it coincidence or serendipity. Call it synchronicity or the hand of God. The people gathered at that time and in that place were a blessed paradigm for a caring community.

Many of us were transient; and perhaps this is a clue to the depth of our experience. Our extended families were thousands of miles away. We relied on our community as our support, mutually filling all the roles of wise elders, loving and scrappy siblings, aunts and uncles to each other's children, safe havens for childcare, respite from boredom, vastly entertaining, witty, intelligent companionship, and a constant source of comfort during times of pain and loss.

When my husband's tour with the US Public Health Service was over and it was time to leave Alaska, I knew that something in me had shifted. For the first time, I was leaving part of myself, something precious, behind. I badly needed to say goodbye and I didn't know how. I was terrified that if one tear escaped, a flood would swamp me and I would drown. There was so much hunger in my soul for all the years of goodbyes that were not said; for all the relationships I allowed to slip away because I could not bear the grief that is part of saying goodbye well. I cried on the plane all the way from Anchorage to Chicago. In case anyone is interested, that is five hours of streaming tears. To some extent that was my worst fear confirmed. Yet the tears were oddly cleansing. The plane did not sink beneath the flood and we arrived safely at our destination.

Not quite conscious of the fact, I was nonetheless learning the first lesson of saying goodbye well. *Tears keep you focused in the present moment.* Tears are the sign of being so aware that all we have is now, that the past is gone, firmly planted where it belongs, and the future has yet to be fulfilled. Tears are a direct pipeline to the heart of the present moment. They are the outward expression of the inner depth of caring and grief. If we are unafraid, the words that flow with them will be the words we need to say to one another. This second lesson, however, was awaiting me a couple of years in the future. Allowing myself to cry was enough for the first go-around.

In our new community in Massachusetts, I had the great privilege of getting to know another doctor's wife, a nurse, who is a warm unselfish woman with compassion to spare. Jean Garnett and I teamed up to start a cancer support group in our local community which soon evolved into our co-founding Shared-Caring Hospice. It should not have been a surprise that I was not finished with my lessons in learning to say goodbye. Week after week as we sat with people ill with cancer and their families, listening to their needs and their stories, I was grateful that I could stay in the present with people who needed that most of all. What I still wasn't prepared for, however, was saying goodbye to new friends I had grown connected to who were never coming back in this lifetime. Someone who is dying deserves so much more from me than *ciao*.

Not only that, I could see that many of us suffered from the same *dis-ease*. Not knowing what to say to someone who is dying is so fearful, so insurmountable that we stop saying anything at all. This isolation of people in the process of living out the end of their days is one of the truly tragic dramas that plays out all around us. If we do manage a visit, we are likely to keep up a stream of chatter about inconsequential matters, or at most inquire about how the person is physically feeling. We say we are "protecting" the dying person from dwelling on morbid thoughts, and the person senses our discomfort and in turn "protects" us, and frequently the family, by not sharing what it is like to know the end is near. The opportunity is lost to be present to one another and to tell each other what isn't being said. Sadly, those are the enormously gifted conversations that enable the living not to fear death.

Almost weekly, I was confronted with the second lesson of saying goodbye well. *Tell the other person how important she has been to you. Tell him how much you value his being in your life.* At the very least we are current with our own feelings and can go away knowing we have said what was in our hearts. More importantly, we aid in creating an atmosphere which honors the experiences and life of the *other* and makes it comfortable and safe for them to freely speak their truth if they choose.

In English *goodbye* comes from the archaic "God be with you," harkening back to a time when even healthy people rarely knew if they would ever see the other person again. Distances and disease, rugged terrains and sudden death all were inimical to long lives and happy endings. When people parted they truly felt that only by the grace of God would they survive long enough to see one another again. To part with a blessing was the sincerest form of caring.

My niece lives in Europe, married to a loving man who comes from a large family in Lebanon. He left his home during the horrors and violence of protracted war seeking a country where he could find economic survival and safety. He explained to me that in his Lebanese family, each time family members left the house, they made the rounds to parents and to each household member kissing them and telling them how much they are loved and valued. If they meet again it will be by the will of the God

"Each time?" I asked.

"Oh, yes. Each time. We learned from the war, you see, by going out on the street to buy food, or to go to school, or to go to work, any of us could be killed or taken. A bomb could destroy our home before we returned. We never knew if this would be the last time we saw our brothers and sisters or our parents. It was very important to say goodbye with love so the last memory will not carry any regrets."

There was the lesson again. *It is very important to say goodbye with love so the last memory will not carry any regrets.*

Alaska taught me the gift of tears. Hospice taught me so much about staying current with my feelings about people and being able to say what those feelings are. The third lesson came about as a natural extension of my professional life.

Part of my job as a trainer for hospice volunteers as well as a psychotherapist was to teach others how to say goodbye. Unfortunately, in psychotherapy we call this "terminating." We terminate with our clients. Horrible word. It always sounded to me that I was about to kill off my client-therapist relationships. At its worst, it connotes a clinical process which encourages me to emotionally distance from clients and hide my feelings behind a professional scientific façade. At its best, it is a word that signifies that there are very real limits to the therapeutic relationship. It is the recognition that for a brief time I-Thou came together for a specific purpose, and now that purpose is fulfilled.

In practice, the word *terminate* is a euphemism for the beneficial healing process of teaching each other how to bring a special connection to its clear, mutually respectful end. In effect I was saying, "We have come this far together; this is where we started; this is what we accomplished along the way; this is where we are. Thank you for the privilege of knowing you and for your trust in sharing part of your deepest self with me for this designated time and purpose. This phase of our relationship is ended; it is terminated."

My third lesson grew out of understanding the importance of this kind of clarity. *Saying goodbye well means taking responsibility for respecting the boundaries of yourself and the other person, as well as the relationship however you define it.* Using the goodbye word with clients is a very different emotional investment from saying the word to loved ones.

The threat of saying farewell to my children and the friends whose love had been such an enormous part of whatever healing had taken place in me, however, caused me to stumble all over my psyche. The last lesson was coming up and I didn't have a clue.

God is not so mysterious. Full of holy mystery? Yes. Mysterious? I don't think so. I had a client once, a tough guy I'll call Bob, who cleared up some holy ambiguities for me. Bob was a tough sweet guy who had spent time in jail when he was a young man. For the past fifteen years he had been straight, sober and mentoring others. He explained to me how he got his huge rage and anger under control.

"Did you ever notice how God throws things at you till you get it? My anger was off the chart, getting me in trouble all the time, even sober. So I reached the point one day when I just gave up and asked my Higher Power to help me with it. I remember it so well. I was in my car at the time. And all the way home one rotten driver after the other cut me off, honked his horn, gave me the finger, almost rear-ended me at a light, and whipped into my parking space right in front of my apartment. I couldn't believe that freakin' ride. I cussed a blue streak for thirty minutes. The veins were popping out in my neck and I just wanted to beat on someone. Anger? I was beside myself. I yelled at God and asked what the hell was going on! I ask for help and what do I get? And you know what?" he asked me.

Fascinated I just had to ask, "What?"

He gave me a quirky little grin, folded his arms across his ample chest and said, "One word loud and clear. PRACTICE!"

"Practice," I repeated, clearly puzzled.

"Yeah. What did I really ask God? I asked for God to take away my anger. Like I was asking God to do the work. And it was like God said, 'OK, you want to get rid of your anger? Here you go, here's your chance. Prove it. Practice not being angry all the way home! '"

I'm not slow. I got it. I'm a mom, and if I could, I would wave a magic wand and dissolve all my kids' issues with life. But what would they learn? My job was to help them find the tools, to *practice* handling their pains. It was my job to provide the opportunities over and over until the tools were their own, just like God. Now here I am, and still "getting it" one more time before I journey away from my life as I have known it.

All those pleadings over all those years: "God, take away my fears about saying goodbye; about grief and leaving and feeling the pain of parting; about feeling abandoned and abandoning; about feeling ashamed of tears which show that I am not in control of my feelings."

I could hear the echo in my soul which sounded strangely like Bob's voice: *Prove it. Here's one more chance to practice.* And isn't that what I had been doing while learning all those lessons? Wasn't God saying, "OK, you want to learn to say goodbye? I'll give you plenty of opportunities to practice." One profound chance after the other to learn to say goodbye well had dropped in my lap. Yet after all this practice I was once again confronted with fears and inadequacies.

The surfacing of old fears was comforting in the paradoxical manner of "better the devil you know." Regression, again, to what is familiar even if it is inhibiting. I knew that eventually, like always, my old self would resurface.

There it was, standing out in the sunshine clear and unadorned. Old Self? My old self barely existed anymore; not the self who bounced merrily from one destination to the other, nor the wife and mother who put her family first before she ever dared think of herself, nor the woman who filled her days and nights with the worries and pains of others. This woman who had packed her whole existence into a nineteen foot camper and cut off her visible means of support, is risking a year of her life on the strength that it is more important to learn how to live from the inside out than to be living a conditioned response to her external world. This woman was a strange new acquaintance.

This new "I" was leaving by choice. There were neither parents nor husband to blame for moving on. I looked into the eyes of beloved children and friends and knew that at this moment I chose to say goodbye. I wanted to say goodbye. There was a rightness to this regardless of its painful ambiguities and its not being purely rational nor sparklingly clear. Through all the long months leading up to this moment, I had never lost the giddy sense of adventure and coming home to something real, alive and juicy in my heart. But the fear that I was irrevocably changing something vital in my self and my relationships haunted that last day. Could it be that I who always thrived on change was now afraid of it?

My definition of change is that nothing can go back to the way things were before. Watching my children grow through their stages into adulthood and being with them through the profound developments of their lives taught me so much about the positive nature of change. Watching my parents grow older, their increased honesty and dignity as they aged have been windows through which I can see the changes in my own future.

Subliminally, I think I was afraid that if I said goodbye, I could never reclaim what was being lost. In deliberately choosing to leave the solace of being part of the everydayness of the lives of those I loved I was irrevocably changing the nature of our relationships. I wanted desperately to be able to go back to saying, "see you later." I wanted the illusion that nothing changes. You and I will still laugh at the same jokes. We will always sing the same songs and read the same books. We will know only the same people and have the same experiences. Time apart will have no meaning. What a sorry fear that is!

Friends and family made this parting time a blessing time. My sons wrestled cartons of personal items into storage while I checked and rechecked the myriads of details involved in handing over my house at the agreed upon moment. Sibling jokes buzzed through the air interspersed with the seriousness of giving mom advice about strangers and roadside behavior. They constantly referred to locking doors and checking in every week.

My oldest son reminded me to *beware of men in tuxedos and women in restrooms.* A poignant reminder of his mortification the first time he flew on his own when he was twelve and I told him to "beware of women in fancy red dresses with flowers in their hair and men in bathrooms." It was my silly attempt to be lighthearted about some very serious concerns. To further my son's incredulity, when we took seats to await his departure, directly across from us was a young woman in a short flame-red dress with a rose tucked behind her ear, chewing gum and swinging her very bare leg. I raised my eyebrows at my son and we roared. The story became part of the family lexicon that routinely got pulled out to illustrate everything from overbearing moms to a great place to pick up dates. He got his point across.

Tears threatened as I laughed off my children's obvious love and concern. How I would miss the repartee and teasing! In their own way they were sending me off with joy and thanksgiving. I closed the door to the house with nothing but laughter ringing in my ears and chuckles lingering in my throat.

I was finished. The work was done. I had nothing left to do but live out the day relaxing with friends and family on the beach and a final farewell dinner. The last two lessons loomed ahead.

I was in awe of the leave-taking, reminding myself to *stay in the present, say what I mean*, and *respect the boundaries of each person*. At the beach I recalled that the many levels of saying goodbye are directly related to the depth of connectedness I felt for each person. In other words, some people were easier to say goodbye to than others. That final afternoon of Labor Day weekend, I discovered that I could be involved in all the goodbye lessons without losing my sense of adventure and anticipation. Over and over people came to me to wish me well, to tell me how exciting my plans were; and many intimated that they would be too frightened to go out in the world alone. Inside I giggled; each question of my journey gave me stronger resolve.

Finally it was time for the last supper and the last two lessons. All my loved ones gathered for dinner at my best friend's house. Each one toasted me and gave me a blessing, gave me per/mission (for the mission) to go and do what I had chosen. I looked around the table at my children, all three in flux, able to provide for themselves yet struggling with the meaning of committed relationships and probably still hurting from their parents' divorce. We talked of the holidays and where and when we would meet. It was unthinkable that we would not be together for Thanksgiving and Christmas. The assurance that the year would not be one of emotional privation cemented the ability to let go.

My friend Christine is the younger sister I never had. She is my other anima, the wholeness of self. She is the gift of reality and authenticity, of spirituality and earthy sensuality. She is the person who aided my navigation through the murky waters of the single life. We had traveled and laughed together and watched with awe the growth of the other. She is that rare person with whom I can be completely myself—no matter who that happens to be at the moment—and accepts me as I am. I knew I would miss her more than I wanted to contemplate. We spoke that last evening of our antics and anecdotes, the places we had been together and about some of the men we had met. Stories were told and laughter shared. When sadness threatened, we reminded ourselves that I would return in a few weeks for her wedding to Marc, one of the world's best men, with which he concurred.

And so the last evening passed and the next to last lesson became clear. *I was free to leave because each person who is important to me had blessed me on my way regardless of how each one felt about what I was doing.* Saying goodbye well meant exactly what the word implied: *God be with you from this moment forward.* This is the most profound, barebones blessing in our language. Goodbye.

When we bless one another, we are saying that we cannot be with each other every moment, we cannot direct each other's lives, and we ultimately can only be responsible *to* not *for,* the other. That is God's job. When I bless you and you bless me, we are as close to unconditional love as we can get in this lifetime. No matter who is leaving and who is staying there are no strings attached, no guilt provoked, and no illusions.

My friends and family gave me the ultimate gift: the freedom to go. And that taught me the last lesson. *When we say goodbye well, we are free to say Hello.*

Book II

Fall:
East Coast

Chapter 5
The Gift of Experience

The day will come when I will be sixty whether I jump into this river of life or not. I will be seventy if I stay in my present circumstance or if I travel out there into unknown places of the world and the soul. I will be eighty with or without the adventure of living from the inside out, learning to be responsible for myself, making choices that would horrify my mother. I will grow older no matter what. I long to grow older making mistakes! Then I will know that I am alive, growing toward something that is the hard won prize of surviving over time. Wisdom is the gift of experience, or so I have been led to believe!
Journal, September

"The first day on the road was as close to terror as I ever want to be!" I wrote in my journal. The camper was not the familiar drive that my beloved little sports car had been. I was unused to checking side mirrors for every turn and stop. I was especially dismayed at the slow response of a cumbersome, top-heavy vehicle that lost momentum going up a simple rise. Having to stay in the right hand lane at the mercy of every murderous truck on the highway pumped my resentment even more. What really eroded my confidence was wondering how I would maneuver that cumbersome rig into camping spots without mowing down people and property. Then I worried in advance about hooking up the water and electricity. Could I do it? Would it work? What would I do if I couldn't manage any of it? Why in heaven's name did I think this was going to be fun? I must be absolutely nuts! Far too nervous to take my hands off the wheel, I dared not put tapes in to listen to music. So, I sang.

I sang every folk song from the sixties and every hymn I could recall from my childhood. Then I went on to sing every recitative, solo and chorus from Handel's *Messiah* that I could remember. I sang until my stomach let go of my heart and my throat ached. I sang until I heard the words one more time, *Look around you, and what do you see?* I sang until I was able to "Be still and know that I am God." I sang until I could once again experience the wonderment of what I was doing and where I was going. I sang until I had to stop for gas and food. Uh-oh.

Today I laugh about how fear took hold when nothing I was doing was familiar or natural. Today I see the absurdity. But on that day, one little question had the power to spiral me into the darkness of panic. On which side of the vehicle was the gas tank? God forbid that I pull up on the wrong side of the pumps. How would I ever get turned around? I couldn't park between those lines at the supermarket, they were too narrow; I'd hit another car! My trip would be over before it began.

When fear took over my focus narrowed by the moment. The more I fed my uncertainties, the smaller my world became until I was in danger of losing sight of the Big Picture, the Reason for Being, the Adventure of Living, the Call of the Inner Voice that had started this whole project. Honestly, the only thing that kept me going at that point was admitting that I had burned my bridges and made my bed. Pride would not allow me to turn around and head for home; not after all the spectacular goodbyes. The unadorned reality was that the only home I had at the moment was the vehicle I was driving. I had no place to go except straight ahead. Maybe this is what those words meant so many months ago when I heard the variation, *straight down the middle.* I had no option but to follow the Voice wherever it led. This was it; I was really out there!

Somewhere near Baltimore, reality of another sort sank in. I was exhausted from the stresses of the last few weeks, not to mention changing my whole life. There were no friends or family to talk to, no one to consult with about what to do next, no one to tell me that I was being courageous, adventuresome, and noble. The reality of driving down the Eastern corridor was far different from standing on the curb in front of my house and asking about right or left. My immediate needs were practical and life-sustaining. I needed a safe place to park and hook-up to electricity so I could eat and sleep.

Pulling into the next rest stop to check maps and campsite locations, I allowed my muscles to relax for the first time in six hours. My attention was snagged, I remember, by several families lunching and bickering at picnic tables, refreshing themselves in the mild September sun. Grandmothers walked their poodles and Chihuahuas, dads yelled at kids who in turn boisterously blasted the air with their Tarzan calls of pent-up energy. Watching those achingly familiar tableaus, my heart hurt as tears of grief caught me unaware. Nose pressed against the window of my own past, I silently screamed for just one more moment of being that wife and mother, whose privilege it was to so carelessly call her family to the everyday feast. I wanted to run to those people and beg, "Pay attention! This moment is precious; it is fleeting! *Be* in this moment, *know* what you have. *Look* at your spouse and your kids and *see* the power in the blessedness and sacredness of it all!"

Shaken to the core, I turned off the engine, let the silence swamp my soul, and welcomed it into that place where bittersweet memories live. That place where those same memories have the power to either charm or harm the present. "How long, O Lord, must I be at the mercy of unwanted feelings that come without volition to haunt the bleakness of my life? How long will it take for me to accept that my old life is over?"

There was an instant of pristine clarity, like sunlight bouncing off a crystal prism surrounding me with colorful dancing lights. It was one of those moments that come like a kick in the pants of consciousness. I knew I was on the threshold of a huge understanding if I only had the courage to open up and let it come. I had the utter certainty that I was literally at the crossroads between choosing to remain stuck in the *desire* for what is past and cannot ever be again, or daring to seek the capacity to redefine my life, memories and all. I could sustain the re-creation of the past by focusing on the memories of what was lost, or I could be about the business of jumping into the pot of cooking up something creative for my next meal. Mrs. Sanford popped into my head.

When I was thirteen I was a mother's helper for the young doctor's wife across the street. She was an exotic French convent-educated Canadian Catholic in our extremely mid-western, puritan protestant community. One of the most fascinating things she did, (besides speaking French, smoking, drinking martinis and dressing formally for *dinner dates* with her own husband in their own candlelit dining room), was the perpetual stockpot she kept on the back burner of her kitchen stove. Every day she added leftover meats and bones as well as vegetables and liquids to this simmering pot. Slimy green things, which I now know were herbs and onion skins swam in the stock like moldy leaves in a puddle, giving me the shivers. Each time I dared a peek, the concoction was a different color. She assured me that the stock she was simmering was rich with the culmination of flavors and nutrients of every meal. Her soups, she said, were outstanding, for nothing was wasted. *"Everything gets better with time and proper attention to the blending."*

Bits of glimmering enlightenment dawned. I would be sitting in the autumn sunshine nostalgically watching young families no matter what my present circumstances: married or alone; traveling or at home. My heaviness of spirit, my inner sadness were not simply about abandonment and loss of husband and identity, they were about the *coming of aging.* That was what it felt like to be simmering with age and experience, to be recognizing that the soup of my life was about all the bits and pieces that **I** had added over the years to make a rich broth that could become the base for so much more. This then is what the books of psychology, philosophy and religion are talking about when they try to explain the importance of integrating all of life's experience into the present moment. I AM the sum total of everything that has come before; and this total, this whole person that sits in the autumn of her life, can only be aware and conscious because *she has lived.*

I have known birth and death. I am intimate with tears and laughter. I am full of the bits and pieces, the slimy and the fresh, the voices of children and the pains of old age, of friends loved and lost, of illness and energy, of plans successfully launched and plans gone awry, of sex and passion, abandonment and hope. My stock would not be as rich as it is if I were not as old as I am. Mrs. Sanford, God bless her, passed on a profound truth. With time and proper blending, everything gets better.

Erik Erikson in his "Eight Ages of Man" says it so well. "It is the acceptance of one's one and only life cycle as something that had to be and that, by necessity, permitted of no substitutions…"[5] This coming of aging which we all face, he intimates, is the acceptance that the life each of us has lived is the only one we have; we cannot go back to make substitutions in the past. Feeling that time is too fleeting to make creative use of what is left, or judging all of life by perpetually recreating the past will hurl us into despair, where we long to escape from the fear of death.

Was this, then, what my sabbatical was to be about, the coming of aging? The growing acceptance that I am finally at a point in life when emerging into the next developmental stage will be far more conscious than at any time previously? Not that I am *old*, but that I am *aware* of the process of growing older. There would be lots of time to figure it out.

I put down my maps and campground literature when I knew where I was headed. With the insights of the moment putting my fears of gas tanks and parking lots in perspective, I headed southeast toward that mystical place of beaches, wild ponies and long lost cousins: Chincoteague Island.

II
Nothing that comes from inside oneself is glib.

The decision to head for Chincoteague was the first road-practicum in following what I had been calling these many months the inner voice. When I looked at the map, my eyes gravitated toward that tiny dot hidden among all the wondrous place names of coastal Maryland and Virginia; places that I knew from books and history and movies. They had names that stirred my sense of adventure by grabbing my attention with their unending possibilities. All of them on the water, all of them supposedly with beaches to accommodate my need for a peaceful place to renew my strength of purpose for the year ahead,which, on that first day, loomed frighteningly, interminably long.

Literally praying for a place where I would feel secure enough to stay until I felt familiar with my equipment, I drove east across a long bridge, holding onto the steering wheel as coastal winds buffeted my ungainly turtle-shell of a home. Traffic thinned and slowed. I drifted through beautiful countryside splashed with rivers and tributaries from the Chesapeake. Names like Cambridge and Salisbury gave me pangs of homesickness for those same places in Massachusetts. I smiled at names like Snow Hill this far south on that warm September day. If I had my way, I would avoid all snow for the coming year. Pocomoke City, however, niggled at my expectations. Here was a name exotically different from what usually fell upon my ears. I saw signs for Temperanceville and laughed out loud as I flashed on a memory of my grandmother's telling me that the only mistake Jesus ever made was turning water into wine. She was a secretary for the Women's Christian Temperance Union (WCTU) in the 1920's. I wondered if she were hovering somewhere nearby, and if she know how eager her errant granddaughter was to toast her first night on the road with a bottle of wine! With such delightfully unholy thoughts making me desperate to find a place, I crossed the causeway into Chincoteague.

I was curious about this small island where the wild ponies lived. I had an uncle who moved here in his retirement from the navy until he died. "Shanghai" they called him. His given name was Harry, but I only knew him as Uncle Dode. He was a distant and romantic figure to me, my brother and our cousins.

There were five boys in my dad's family. One died in adolescence, three were ministers or preachers, and one was a wild sailor boy who joined up after high school and spent most of his time out of the country. He was reputed to have been on the Yangtze River when the Japanese took over mainland China, and later became a submariner during the Second World War. According to my grandma, it was while he was interred beneath the deep that he was forced to drink. "Lookee here! They made those sailors drink alcohol to keep them quiet," she blithely explained away this aberration in our teetotalling family. I was enthralled. He probably smoked, too.

My one and lovely memory of him was the time he came home on leave and brought me the most exquisite stuffed puppy. My daddy was overseas at some place called The Burma Road and I had not seen him for two years. To have my uncle pick me up, hug me and give me a present was a gift so precious I had never forgotten.

After the war, dad came home to the full-time pastorate and Uncle Dode stayed on as a career sailor. Stories of his life flourished at Thanksgiving when all the siblings met at Grandma Rose's house. In truth, we kids envied Dode's exciting life. It was so much more romantic than being a preacher's kid. In later years, in retirement, he and my dad stayed in closer touch, but I was long gone from home. Now Uncle Dode was gone and I had two much younger cousins living somewhere in the vicinity, perhaps.

Can the psyche get tired, I wondered? All those memories stirred up by one trip down the highway were leaving me with a weariness more deep than simple tiredness from the journey. I knew that this was not random, just as the memories at the rest stop were not. If I were going to be true to living from the inside out, then I had to be true to the knowledge that for some reason yet to be discovered, I was looking at the bits and pieces in my stockpot. It was definitely time to get off the road.

Getting through the small downtown of Chincoteague, I continued east toward Assateague Island National Seashore, where, I discovered, there were no campgrounds on the beaches with hookups for electricity and water. There went my first expectation. However, there was a sparkling private campground very near the entrance to the National Seashore area in Chincoteague. Tall southern pines shaded uncrowded, grassy camp sites complete with table and hookups. Several small shops and food stores were near the entrance. A few feet to the east, biking and hiking trails meandered for three miles through a wooded parkland that was home to the wild ponies, ending at the beachfront on

Assateague where the sand stretched forever. At last, a place to make my bed and eat, with access to the beach and the ocean. My weary soul sighed.

The woman behind the desk in the office was surprised when I stated that there was only one person asking for accommodations. "You're by yourself?" she asked, checking me out. "We had a single woman in here once, earlier this season. But she was pretty young. A real character. Towed a Mercedes behind her rig."

There wasn't much I could say to this conversation stopper, so I assured her that I, too, had character but no Mercedes. "She got *real* friendly with folks in town." This was delivered with a knowing look. "Said she was traveling to California for a new job. Wanted to *experience* as much of the country as she could along the way." This was tossed out with a sly snort.

Too tired to assure her that I would not be having wild orgies in my van, as arresting a thought as that was, I simply said, "Really."

Clearly I was a curiosity in her mind and she was searching for a frame of reference, a peg on which to hang me. "How far did you come?" In my current state, that was a complex question.

"Massachusetts," I answered while I filled out her forms and tried to get in touch with my inner self. Her questions and observations were distracting me from my listening stance. She was asking me to pay in advance for the number of nights I wanted to be in residence, but I couldn't *hear* a definitive answer. I had not had a chance to ask, *How long?* Listen, trust, act. Where were they when I needed them?

Had I really expected minute-by-minute to hear answers to my questions ringing like a crystalline bell of Evensong filling up my internal landscape? For the briefest of moments, doubt intruded until I chased it away with a resurgence of affirmation. Yes, that is exactly what I expected and trusted. Obviously I needed to work on how to conduct life in the external world while simultaneously listening to direction from the inside. I was feeling so raw and vulnerable, so out of my depths, so unprepared for the realities of what I was embarking upon.

When I confessed to the owner of the campground that this was my first stop on a year-long journey, that I had no idea how long I would stay, she immediately shed her intrusive questioning in exchange for shared feminine support. For my security, she suggested a spot near the bathhouse restroom that was also within spotting distance of the office with its 24-hour surveillance system. We would work out the payment as time evolved.

Grateful for her kindness and guilty for my judgment of her seemingly gossipy nature, I did not yet realize that two significant themes had just been introduced that would play out for the rest of the year.

1.—my age and single state invited curiosity and unsolicited personal commentary that couples or families rarely got

2.—the more honest, authentic and real I became, the greater the chance of being responded to in kind

Curiosity and support proved to be the touchstones of each and every place I landed. Put another way, the earthy and the divine sang a duet in my ear and in my heart everywhere I went. But for that first night, I was simply relieved to pull into my spot without incident.

As evening descended, the sky showed a lowering band of apricot barely visible through the lush vegetation of pines and coastal bushes. Still warm with a hint of on-shore breeze, the day slowly slipped toward evening as I sat in my folding chair mesmerized by the symphonic sounds of a southern twilight as the world closed down. I breathed in the sounds of cicadas and crickets singing the last songs of the day. Earth-animals burrowed in for the night causing leaves to rub together and pine needles to fall with little rustles and clicks. I allowed the peacefulness to sink into my center while my eyes feasted on the beauty. I let my soul rejoice.

Open your eyes, I heard, *and see your new living-room.* A giggle started low in my belly. My new living-room! Look at it! Such depth, such color, such co-ordination and harmony. I raised my glass of wine and toasted my Divine Decorator. "Thank you. Thank you for all of this and for one more chance to give my *living, room.*

III

How strange it was to wake up in a sofa bed that took up the whole central area of a camper normally used as a living-room, where the lounge chair was the passenger seat turned around, and the kitchen was literally an arm's length away. It was perfect for flicking the switch on the coffee pot while lying in my bed. A small shift and the refrigerator gave up its milky contents. Bacon and coffee smells invaded from outside, as well as the sounds of other campers gearing up for the day. I lay there contemplating the ceiling, impatient for coffee, letting my thoughts meander.

My first day.

My first real day camping.

This is what I came to do.

Yes. I have the whole day before me.

I can do anything I want.

I have no schedule. I have no more black book. I have no more calendar.

I am free.

I can do anything I want.

I can go where I please.

Yes.

I have a whole year of this wonderful freedom and peace.

Yes.

I can do anything I want. By this time I was twiddling my thumbs.

Cautiously I tweaked the slats on the blinds over my bed so I could look out. The sun was shining. I should get out there. I should go to the curb and ask which direction to go. I was in Chincoteague, Virginia. I should get out and see the town. Or I could stay right there in my van, safe and snug with lots of coffee and lots of books.

Yes. I could do anything I wanted.

The enormity of my total independence and isolation hit me. What was it that I *wanted* to do?

That was perhaps the first time in my whole fifty plus years that I had asked that question when there were no expectations of what the answer would be. I was on the journey to discover how to live from the inside out, and on the first day I had to admit that I honestly did not foresee beyond the point of getting on the road. The trip itself had always been in that murky cloudy place of it-will-be-such-a-great-trip. I had not tried to realize what the day-to-day deal would be. All my energies had been expended on getting to this point. Now I had to deal with the *now*, and contrarily I missed my unholy trinity with desperation. What would take the place of appointment book, calendar and checkbook? The first two I had thrown out with abandonment, and the last was unnecessary because I had made arrangements to pay my bills by direct payment from the bank. What would structure my life? Not even out of bed on the first day and I was having a crisis of identity.

Then I remembered the joy of my new living-room and the absolute delight I felt in pushing out the walls of my *preconceived* ideas about the rooms in which living takes place. Put in this context, I realized that everything about this trip so far had blown away my expectations and preconceptions. In fact, there was nothing about the present circumstance that in any manner met any criteria, expectation or preconception about who, what, where or when would be right and in place for me at this time in my life.

I was supposed to be looking forward to the financial and emotional advantages of an enduring faithful partnership/ marriage and planning for a carefree retirement, as *we* happily awaited the advent of weddings and grandchildren. I was supposed to be blessedly accepting the many fruits of many labors, and reaping the rewards of tax-sheltered benefits. None of those preconceived ideas were in truth a part of my present reality. I was not supposed to be in a camper alone at the Virginia seashore!

The previous day's swamp of memories began to make a weird kind of sense in at least two ways. Holding onto memories in order to prove a certain perception limits my ability to grow beyond the pain of disappointments and regrets. It creates the kind of history that perpetuates keeping the hurt alive, justifying anger and blocking the paths to reconciliation and integration. The coming of aging is in part coming to terms with memory; letting go of the parts that are non-nutritive and keeping with quiet joy the parts that add to my succulent soup base.

And secondly, I had to take a long look at the specificity of the memories. Yesterday had been a trip of stupendous import. I traveled geographically, and intrapsychically tripped, through my whole lifetime from childhood to the edge of aging. In the light of the insight about memories and letting go, Uncle Dode did not seem to fit. In a sense I never had him. That is, he was not a central or dominant figure in any way in my life. He was that mysterious mythical character most families can relate to in some fashion. Whatever his own personal truth, to me he was daringly out-in-the-world risky as well as fun-loving and strong. I endowed him with the strength to be able to live life on his own terms. He was my only familial archetypal warrior. Was it coincidence that I was led to start my year's journey in that place where Uncle Dode lived and died? I think not. In my soupcon of memories, in my collective unconscious gene pool, his perceived qualities were the ones I would need not only for the year ahead, but for living the sometimes harsh truths of aging.

Truth 1—Give up all preconceived ideas; keep a mind open to new possibilities.

Truth 2—Dare to shake loose from the ruts of security by venturing into new territory of the soul.

Uncle Dode personified the protector, the Viking, the one who had the courage to venture forth. No wonder I dredged him up in my daydreams. I needed him.

What other rooms were in store for me if I were to get out of bed and explore my space? Listen. Trust. Act. The time had come. The voice that I had cultivated so determinedly was waiting. Life was just beginning. Again.

Chapter 6
Beaches: in the Beginning

Salt Grasses

I don't know much, but this I know:
Where sand meets sky the grasses grow.
The grasses grow in sea-salt air
And ring the dunes like maidens' hair.

Like maidens' hair the grasses sway
Uncombed, uncut, unbound for play.
And play they do, I know that much,
Where sand and sea and sky can touch.
Journal: Chincoteague, VA September

I loaded up the panniers on my bicycle with the usual beach necessities, bungeed a beach chair and towel on the rear fender, and suddenly obsessed about leaving all my possessions behind in my camper which anyone could break into. If someone got my travelers checks, I was finished! I dashed back inside one more time to check that my safe, which was hidden in plain view, still held my stash, that it really couldn't be identified as anything other than the condiment box it was designed to look like. Standing there in my bathing suit cover-up, baseball cap and tennis shoes ready for my big adventure to the beach, the ludicrous picture I made in my mind's eye undid me. I laughed until

I could hardly breathe, then saluted my safe and walked out locking the flimsy door behind me. What was the worst thing that could happen?

The vision that sustained me through the long months of preparation and planning was that God would honor my quest for learning to live from the inside out. The logical progression of aha's and epiphanal moments had taken me from the simple hunger for change through the undeniably transformational process of allowing my inner spiritual voice to become the one that dictated my thoughts and actions, to following where that voice led. The next step, it appeared, was to cleanse my mind and feelings of preconceptions internalized over a lifetime, the result of reacting to my external world. This is what my friend, Lin, calls our *good girl syndrome*. Like many women of my generation, I was programmed to react to the external stimuli of what other people needed from me. Now it was time to learn about the world from the inner perspective of personal responsible choice. The only way I could conceive of learning to do this was to immerse myself in the place where all life began; where sea and sand and sky came together.

How strange that felt; how out of my element. I was a lake and pools girl. Beaches were so unmanageable. They were too hot on the feet and annoyingly scratchy under the bathing suit. Beaches are too dangerous for the skin and terribly uncomfortable unless you find a way to transport half the contents of your house. I had endured the local ones over the years for my kids' sake, and for socializing. I didn't want to miss anything. I have to admit that if I'm comfortable, I love the soul bending views of horizons and water.

The first half of my life I grew up landlocked in Kentucky and Ohio. There were lakes, rivers and creeks aplenty for swimming, fishing and dunking. Lake Erie was nearby for getting an occasional metaphysical jab, a haunting reminder of the relative fragility of our puny species juxtaposed to the vast imposing powers of Nature's waterways. It was moving to New England that taught me the difference between inviting the lake into my life for the occasional getaway, and living in an area near the sea.

The ocean is not only a huge external force, it is an unconscious presence circumscribing life everyday. It influences weather, the local smells and terrain, and certainly the food. It dictates local economic realities, education, and recreation. It promotes spirituality, art, family time, dating rituals and traffic patterns. Its claim on those born in the area is so profound that most natives will tell you that no matter where they move in the world, they have salt water in their veins. They cannot exist permanently away from access to the sea.

When I was new to the area, I heard all this as exclusionary. I couldn't possibly belong here if I weren't born here. Over time, however, I had come to realize that peoples' relationship to the ocean is as simple and complex as its being part of their identity. I had heard the same sentiment from people born in the desert and the mountains or plains. It is as though in some folks there is primal atavistic knowledge that we are all intrinsically connected to that part of the earth where we were born. We are the tangible proof that God picked up the bits and pieces of water, or clay, or schist and breathed the breath of life into it.

I may not have been born near the water, but I was not immune to its pull or to the seduction of its tangy perfume that tingled the nose by riding on the breezes of summer afternoons. There is something primordial in the tug of the ocean when its waves pound the shore where eddying tidal waters leave behind the evidence of the first births of the land. This, I knew instinctively, was what I needed. This was what I was yearning for that cold January day in Massachusetts nine months ago. The hunger went far deeper than relaxing, or reading a book on the beach while soaking up the sun and praying for no strap marks.

Everything in me was urging me toward the beach. Not a frantic *have to* but an exciting *going to*. This time, I was approaching with an intentionally cleaner slate, opening up my mind and my heart to starting over, and erasing the nit-picking tidbits of past experience that limit my imagination.

Stepping out of my little box of anxiety about someone helping themselves to my personal goods while I was at the beach was freeing. Campers compose one of the most trustworthy communities in our culture. But it would take me several more weeks before I began to relax enough to leave my doors unlocked if I weren't in the immediate vicinity. Knowing that I was as secure as I could be, I got on my bike.

With each turn of the wheels my heart flew higher. The day was perfect. Sunny, mild and just enough breeze from the distant ocean to make the ride a joy. *Look at me! I'm here! I'm riding my bike through the Reserve at Chincoteague!* Somewhere in the back of my head a voice piped up: *Is this enough change yet?* I loved it. This was about as far from my over-scheduled life as I could get. I wallowed in the joy and freedom of a simple ride through an enchanted forest. My senses were heightened by the peacefulness of over-arching trees, where the songs of birds rose like prayers in a cathedral.

Just as I thought that I could not worship any more, off in the distance was a small herd of the wild ponies for which the island is famous. Munching grass and seemingly oblivious to my encroaching bicycle, one or two of them raised their heads checking to see if I posed any danger. I found myself thanking them for sharing their home with me and asking permission to ride through their dining room.

I shocked myself silly with these childish fantasies. Self-consciousness reared its chastising voice with reminders of acting my age. Then another thought occurred. *You asked to be connected. You asked to live from the inside out. Do you think maybe this is part of seeing the world with new eyes? Part of starting over? Is this what it's like to get rid of preconceived ideas?*

As the last of this question faded away, I leaned into a curve and there in the middle of the path was a full-sized deer, not moving, just looking straight at me with no fear. It was as though I had asked the last questions out loud. She tilted her head slightly and then very slowly nodded her head three times as if she were saying, "Yes, yes, and yes," before she quietly walked off the path and into the brush leaving a somewhat stunned but very humbled person behind.

The ride to the beach was a first in meditative biking. Breathing in the tangy air, I allowed the noise of the world to drop away, asking only to be in the present moment and let the inner knowing be the guide. As always, there was the swing between the sublime and the ridiculous. This wondrous feeling of spiritual lightness gave way immediately when I struggled with my egregious amount of equipment across the sands to lay claim to the most pristine spot as my own territory. Relatively few people populated the beaches after Labor Day.

Despite my spiritual high, the old familiar insecurities came to life so faithfully that it scared me. I found myself saying, "Slow down." Those critical superego voices of the past which loved to whisper old messages of not being perfect enough to disrobe in public had no place here. Breathing deeply I made a conscious choice to let thoughts of cellulite and sagging breasts blow away with the breeze and made a dash for the shoreline. I wanted to be more graceful than that. No. I chose to be more graceful than that.

Why did our ancestors think the world was flat? Assateague beach was surrounded by an over-arching sky that kissed the earth at the horizons of sand and water. Like a perfect crystal bowl set over a plate, the dome of heaven arced overhead while I stood listening to the world with my eyes as well as my ears. I was exactly where I was supposed to be, alone at the edge of the world, crawling out of the water, taking my first autonomous breath, and forging my own footprints in the sand. Everything felt ancient and metaphoric, like the old ones talk of Body Wisdom. That day I was participating in my own birth.

I did not hum a mantra. There was no need for the reminder to be still and know who is God. Next to the pounding of the waves and the hugeness of the skies, I was like a grain of sand, part of the pattern but not the center of the world. There was much to learn before I could leave this place.

The child in me played with purpose, running in and out of the waves while strengthening legs, developing muscles of the soul for the adventures still to come. I walked for miles like the adolescent who wants to go as far and as fast as she can to test the limits of her own vulnerability.

All around me I saw patterns. The waves whooshed in a little higher each time. Each time they receded they left ripples in the sand, geometrically pleasing. Waving grasses wove together creating wall hangings against the dunes. And everywhere the shells, each one unique, made complicated collages on the sandy canvas.

Wrapping all was nature's surround sound as the concert of the beach echoed the music of a universe at work and play. Gulls screeched and dove for the same bits of food, arguing with their tern cousins over feeding rights, while the castanets of crabs clawing quickly out of reach spiced up the tune. Underneath it all the booming tide was a reminder that there are some things in this world, like the tides, that are immutable, reliable and forever.

That was what I came here to this specific beach to learn. That is why I came to the edge of this primordial world, old as Time, rooted and grounded in the ebb and flow of evolving strength and ancient wisdom. Connectedness was far greater and far deeper than feeling close to people and places I loved and wanted to be with. Connectedness is *knowing* I am a part of everything, and that everything is part of me. *I am never alone.* I have a place in the world. That is what I was led here to see.

Riding back to the camper my psyche was on overload. I smiled and said hello to people hiking toward me and was startled to realize that I had gone the whole day without speaking to another person.

A couple from Ohio asked to see my van. They were renting a small RV, but had long been interested in a Falcon, like mine. They seemed a little startled when they observed that I had managed to pack a guitar, keyboard, books and computer in a very compact space designed for a meager amount of clothing and food. I proudly showed them how I had the bathroom converted into a basket-filled closet to remedy the storage problem. After all, I reasoned, campgrounds have bathroom facilities, so why take up important storage space in the camper that could be more efficiently used. The bathroom was only thirty-six inches wide with a chemical toilet and a hand-held shower head. The hot water tank held about two gallons of water which would not be enough to wash my hair let alone the rest of me. And emptying the refuse holding tank was not something I wanted to contemplate. So I had no problem with gathering up my toiletries and clean clothes and heading off to the shower room. It was all a matter of priorities.

The Ohioans smiled and thanked me for the tour, leaving me with the thought that I had told them things they would just as soon not have known. I did not have to compensate for not talking all day by talking the ears off the first people I met. I wonder what I did for Falcon sales.

At sundown, a woman stopped by to chat and I invited her to sit and share a glass of wine. We did what women do so well. We connected by sharing our personal histories, or at least as much as was appropriate to the evening. We gently roamed the topic of commitment, and she shared how hard she has worked all her life while honoring her primary relationships. The sun dropped out of sight leaving us in that mellow place at the end of the day when tiredness takes over and we more readily speak our minds. She envied my chance to travel this year. Yet I knew it was not the travel she envied. It was the freedom of choice.

"And what would you like to do?" I asked her. "What would you do if you felt you could?" Her answer was the answer of so many women I have listened to over the years.

"I don't know. I've never *dared* think about *just me.*" We let her words sit in the space between us as we quietly contemplated the distance while slowly sipping our wine.

She stood up to walk away, then turned around and said, "We've really covered a lot of topics haven't we?" This was asked with the quiet pride of someone who is wistfully surprised at being heard in a mutual exchange. I agreed. She kept walking and turned again from farther away, leaning intensely into the question. "That's really *good,* isn't it?" I smiled and nodded. "Yes, it is. *Really* good. Thank you for spending time with me." Once again she turned and came part way back.

"I don't even know your name." I told her.

She said, "My name is Ida Harp." With quiet dignity, she walked into the night leaving me with a heart full of gratitude and quiet joy for the gifts that were coming my way.

So many connections, so many surprises. Ida was my grandmother's name, the very one who couldn't wait to get to heaven to ask Jesus what on earth he thought he was doing encouraging demon alcohol. I lifted my glass skyward and got a giggle out of wondering if Ida and Dode were both around and what they found to talk about.

Sitting alone in the fading light, I thought that it was time to retreat into the close security of my Falcon, my little shell of a home, to turn on the lights and settle in. Not for the first time I compared myself to the turtle or the snail living within the confines of a preternatural space, all the while dimly aware of how much room there was, if not for the body, for the soul to grow.

The words of a poem floated through my head teasing my unreliable memory, energizing me to leave my outdoor contemplations and wine to close down for the night. Surely in all the books I packed, somewhere in the piles of stuff I thought I could not live without, there must be a volume that contained those words. Perfect poetic words. I had to read those words. Quite determined to find the poem, I plowed through books and drawers, unmindful of the tiny space that I was literally littering. When I found it, I sank down to the floor and braced the book against my bent knees to read Oliver Wendell Holmes' *The Chambered Nautilus.*

Holmes was inspired by the beauty of the pearly nautilus, a mollusk, which each year builds a new chamber in its shell. Year after year the little creature adds another pearlized spiral to its domain so that as it ages his space becomes ever more vast and beauteous until the end of its time. But it was the last verse that has stayed with me through the years.

Build thee more stately mansions, O my soul,
As the swift seasons roll!
Leave thy low-vaulted past!
Let each new temple, nobler than the last,
Shut thee from heaven with a dome more vast,
Till thou at length art free,
Leaving thine outgrown shell by life's unresting sea![6]

Connection, growth, leaving, arriving, spinning out the seasons of life that inevitably lead to freedom. Sitting on the floor of my van, huddled in my shell, I had hope that life was not over. This business of building stately mansions of the soul would be the great task of the last third of my life. The fears and worries of being old were just that, fears and worries. The realities were that the great adventures of the inner life were just beginning. Perhaps one of the purposes for being where I was at that moment was to record the stories of the people I was meeting. They were leaving patterns in the sand of my life.

Preparing for bed was a chore when there were piles of books and papers scattered over the living room which, out of necessity, became the bedroom. I turned out the light and tried to get comfortable while contemplating the events of the last 24 hours. The very firm mattress that is the couch by day just might turn out to be a real thorn in the flesh. It was better than a tent, I adjured myself. I planned to adjust. I attempted to put the day into perspective as all the insights, the highs, the surprises, and the connections played havoc with my sleep hormones. I centered. I prayed. I meditated. I rolled over and then back again. Finally, I said one last prayer. "Please, God, can I lighten up tomorrow? Can I just have some fun?"

Chapter 7
Sand Patterns

Unseen Friend

See the patterns in the sand
Painted by an Unseen Hand.
Perchance a Navajo passed this way
Transcending time and space today.

One great mosaic is this earth
Where every tiny part has worth:
The shell, the child, the crab, the tree
By grand design are part of me.

If I am part of all I see
What binds my unseen friend to me?
The Artist paints the sand, the dove;
Connects us with the color Love.
Journal: Edisto Island, SC, November

Someone in the Southern Hemisphere must have instituted January as the beginning of the New Year. Those of us who live in the Northern Hemisphere, however, know that autumn is the true beginning of each year. January is simply an excuse for those of us in cold climates to have a party during the mid-winter blahs. Nothing new really begins at that time of year. Mostly we are hanging-on until the leisurely days of summer roll round. Like the great epics, the January New Year starts *en medias res:* in the middle of things. It is the middle of the work year, the academic year, the family year. Toward spring and summer we wind down by changing our schedules and incorporating more barbecues. It's an excuse to suspend our regular work-outs and committee meetings. We make plans to visit, travel, go to the beach, or invite our best friends with all the kids to our house. Finally, August drains summer like the last sip of fine champagne. One more swallow would be too much, but the last tart bubble is nostalgically savored as we reluctantly let go of what was, for what will be. Then September arrives and reinvigorates us for work and purpose.

In September, we start as we mean to go on—until the next nirvana summer. When the sea winds bear a cooler breeze, the mountain air freshens and the leaves of autumn glow, we store the fruits of summer and energetically make plans for the rest of the year. So it was that in the autumn of my life I took stock of the delicious harvests stored in the quiet places of my root cellar in preparation for the next stage of the journey.

All that fall, from September to December, I roamed the beaches of the Eastern seaboard, traveling as far south as the Florida Keys, staying in each place until, by diligent listening, I knew that it was time to move on. The sun drew me from Chincoteague to Hatteras Island, NC, down to South Carolina's Charleston and Edisto Island; then to Sea Island and Jekyll Island, Georgia; and finally to Key Largo, Bahia Honda and Key West in Florida.

How deliciously seductive it was wearing bathing suits and shorts long after Labor Day. I was still deepening my tan at the end of summer and reveling in the freedom from cold weather and fuel bills. Yet there lingered a niggling sense of unease that I was sticking too close to home. Why was I not bound for California, or Montana, or North Dakota? No inner urge or internal dialogue pried me loose from the water with all its mystery and power. I was forced to contemplate, that long freeing fall, that my sabbatical might never take me any deeper into the interior parts of my country. A metaphor for life, I ruminated in the dark hours of the night. Perhaps my soul was so parched for living waters that it would take the entire year to drink my fill and I would never be directed to mountains and deserts.

Or was it more prosaic? Was I simply not yet ready to venture too far beyond the physical reach of my children and friends? Weekly phone calls gave me the illusion that I was still in the neighborhood. Without this grounding, this affirmation of my very identity, who would I be? Or was I being forced to look at the depths of commitment and what it means?

"Wanna' walk with us to the water, Miss Jean?" Billy, the surfer-dressed seven-year old, yelled into my door. His freckles fairly danced across his nose. "Me and Terry's goin' to the beach and Momma says you might like to walk with us." As the mother of sons, I recognized accomplished manipulators when I met them.

"Are you sure it's okay with your Mom?" I asked with some skepticism. Being the caretaker of children swimming in the ocean seemed a huge liability a mother wouldn't lightly pass off.

"Yes, Miss Jean," dimpled big nine-year-old brother Terry. "We got us our kites. We don't wanna' go in the water. We just wanna' fly our kites. Momma don't care. She'll be along soon as she gets everthin' set up." He had that total masculine assurance that I would fall in with any plans he so earnestly assumed.

Armed with my agreement, those little southern charmers convinced their harassed mother that they would be gentlemen and mind Miss Jean, if only Momma would allow them to go to the beach now and not have to wait for her to finish cleaning up and dressing the baby.

The wind and surf were up, the dunes high, and the sky so blue my mouth watered. The boys were right. It was a perfect time and place for kite flying. Billy and Terry were no novices. They had those kites up and smacking against the wind in no time, whooping and hollering in that unrestrained way kids have when they are totally unselfconscious. Up the kites flew, then suddenly dived dangerously toward the sand on a downdraft. Screaming at one another the brothers competed for the heights and endearingly encouraged each other in the lows. I sat on the dune watching them with nothing but joy in the moment, basking in the cleansing immediacy of childhood.

Inevitably, the little guy tripped and the string flew out of his hand. He watched in disbelief as his golden kite, freed from its anchor, danced out of reach. We both dashed for the trailing string. Too late! Too late! The capricious winds whisked Billy's kite just out of reach, then on a great gust sent it up, up until it was absorbed by the blue where we could no longer see it. Billy's grief and loss were as unselfconscious as his joy had been just moments before. It was the most natural thing in the world to pull him onto my lap to comfort him.

"It's gone! It's gone, Miss Jean! It's not fay-er!" Billy sobbed.

No, it wasn't fair. But how do you talk to a seven year old about the universal inequities of life, especially when his big brother continues to whoop it up down the beach? "No, sweetheart, it's not fair." I rested my cheek against his hair, half-way undone by the little boy smells of sweat and sweetness.

"I don't like that ole kite, anyways!" How quickly we learn to displace our hurts. "I hate him!"

"That's too bad," I say to Billy. "It looked to me like that ole kite was giving you a good time for a while there." I sighed dramatically, "I guess he just had other plans, other places he had to go. It was time for him to move on." A long pause.

"Where'd he go?" came the little voice from my lap.

"Oh, I don't know for sure. He went in that direction." I point out over the water. "What do you think lies over that way?"

"China," he said unequivocally, "I think he went to China, Miss Jean. All the way to China." He sat up with the force of his certainty.

"You could be right, Billy." I tried to invest my voice with all the seriousness the situation warranted. "I wonder what will happen to him there?"

I assumed Billy's silence treated my question as rhetorical, until he spoke up again.

"He'll come down when he gets ready." Warming to his subject,

Billy jumped on his knees. "Maybe he'll find another little boy and play on that beach in China—."

"Maybe he will. That's a great idea."

"—and then that little boy will fall and my kite will go away again, and then he'll keep goin' 'til he comes down again, and then he'll find a little boy, and then he'll fly away again, and then, you know what?" Billy's little perfect body quivered with his insights.

"What?" I asked breathlessly, as anxious as he to discover the meaning of life.

"He'll come right back home here and find me a-gay-in." In his new found vision, the little Teacher dropped the *maybes*.

Billy's tears dried up as he excitedly contemplated the cyclical mysteries of the universe, while mine were clogging my throat. "Maybe he will, Billy, maybe he will." And I prayed that it was so.

Long after Billy and Terry vacated the beach with their Momma and the baby, I was left with a full heart, pondering the exquisite Mary Moment when innocence gave voice to wisdom. The sun was still golden, the heavens were still intensely blue, yet everything had a slightly different cast as things do when truth is both spoken and heard in the authentic self. I licked my finger and held it aloft, testing the direction of the air currents. When will you come, O Wind, to tug the string loose from my hand and send my kite soaring? Or is it my choice to merely let go?

During my walks I began to *see* the infinite variety of wonder-full patterns on the beach. Thousands of shells wash up on the sands of the Sea Islands. Large, small, intact and fragmented; some bleached by sun and salt, others darkened by aging kelp. But that is not all the beach has in store. There are fabulous fossils: sharks teeth, mastodon teeth and bones. Varieties of Native American pottery shards worn smooth by time, give rise to rich imaginings of life lived before anything known to those of us fortunate to be walking here today. The striations left on the sand by receding waters washing over this infinite variety of "outworn shells" reminded me of the interwoven patterns I had seen in Navajo rugs. Designs aptly named Eyedazzler and Tree of Life by generations of artists.

I sat in the foaming tide where the surging waters tumbled these riches and watched the hand of God weaving in the universe. My heart beat with the pounding of the surf and for one perfect second I knew down to my bones that I am a part of all that is seen and unseen. *Existence is a grand mosaic.* I have had this thought before, but this time it went beyond intellect to the heart of *being.* It went to the heart of death and resurrection, transporting me beyond the fears of human frailty and time passing. The thought excited me with the surety that everything and everyone has worth in the connectedness of the Divine Plan. Watching the ocean in its dynamic pursuit of the raising and lowering of water levels, I thought about the intricate workings of moon and water over the course of each month.

There was no one left on the beach when I lay on my back, spread-eagled at the ocean's edge, loving the feel of being part of the endless rhythm, and anxious to see if my body will leave its pattern on the shore. It occurred to me that women, ancient, mythic and modern are especially in tune with the tides. We flow with the moon cycles, ever-changing, in-out, up-down. At some level of our Source we intrinsically understand the natural force and flow of our lives. Like the sea we are in the flow of cyclical movement where the only surety is that all is flux.

I watched the shore, the waves breaking far out then hitting the sand with such force that the spray shot into the air. Then spent, it was ready to recede and regroup. Over and over, powerful and majestic, the sea is in absolute harmony with what it was created to do and to be. The sea has no self-consciousness, no struggle with "am I doing the right thing? Is this where I belong? Is this all I am called to do or to be?" The sea *is.* How much more joy there would be in my living if I experienced the certitude of my place in the pattern as clearly. Simply *being.*

Of course, looking back, I see that from September to December I was solidifying my purpose, *screwing my courage to the sticking place*, as Shakespeare urged, getting comfortable in my new skin by giving myself time to evolve. The uncovering of truths within and making the life-changes necessary for living out of those truths are two different kettles of soup. Insights can be an awesome emotional and spiritual high. But if they are not connected to the grittier realities of daily life, they too easily evaporate. I needed time to practice my insights which seemed absolutely key to turning my life inside-out, as well as coming to terms with my own very human and fallible nature. I needed time to kick some old habits and pick up new ones. I needed time to experience my own patterns in the sand.

Chapter 8
Distractors and Enhancers

"Dear Wormwood: [novice Tempter]

Work hard, then, on the disappointment or anticlimax which is certainly coming to the patient during his first few weeks as a churchman. The Enemy [God] allows this disappointment to occur on the threshold of every human endeavor...It occurs when the boy who has been enchanted in the nursery by Stories from the Odyssey buckles down to really learning Greek. It occurs when lovers have got married and begin the real task of learning to live together. In every department of life it marks the transition from dreaming aspirations to laborious doing... Desiring their freedom, He therefore refuses to carry them, by their mere affections and habits, to any of the goals which He sets before them: He leaves them to "do it on their own." And there lies our opportunity...

Your affectionate uncle,
Screwtape"
(Retired Demon)
from C.S. Lewis, The Screwtape Letters[7]

One pattern that emerged, a horrible habit indeed, was elementary in its obviousness, practically a cliché. It had to do with the old law about every action having an opposite and equal reaction. Anyone who has ever determined to start a diet or give up other destructive behaviors can easily understand what this means. Those of you who make up your mind to stick to a budget, or commence a spiritual path know exactly what I am talking about. As soon as the thought forms in the head we are almost immediately invited to be a food judge for the county fair, hit the biggest cashmere sweater sale of the century, are offered endless opportunities to drink, smoke or swear, or are tormented by the exhausting details of everyday life that demand undivided attention every waking moment. Add to this the other cliché about taking yourself with you wherever you go and a defeatist picture begins to form.

You can label this *law* with any name you want: my-cross-to bear or resistance. It doesn't matter. The unwritten law of the universe declares that whenever we strive for the highest and the best, it is inevitable that all our foibles and follies will crash in on us like a storm at high tide. That is what Bob was trying so eloquently to explain to me months ago when he described the agonies of making a commitment to dealing with his anger. Was I ever learning in a condensed and focused manner the subtleties and complexities of this Universal Law! The more determined I became to be inwardly focused and spiritual, the greater were the distractions that conspired to keep my attention on the external and the earthy.

My intentions were good. Sure they were lofty. But they were edifying and absolutely fundamental to making changes in behavior, thought and prayer. In order to live from the inside out, I figured I needed to structure a daily discipline much as I had been doing the previous year. The exception was that it would not be rushed nor fit into an over burdened schedule. It would be more, well, *intentional*, with the added luxury of performing each part every day for as long as was needed. I made a sign and posted it in my camper just in case I was tempted to forget what I was about:

EVERYDAY INTENTIONS
1. **Prayer and meditation: listen, trust, act; read inspirational literature**
2. **Journal writing: insights from prayer and meditation; daily log, events, people, interpretations, thoughts, writing ideas**

3. **Exercise: walking, biking, breathing, swimming**
4. **Healthy eating: plan meals, balanced diet, good supply of snacks on hand (healthy!)**

Very simple, very elemental, and, according to behavioral psychology, everything on the poster was necessary for a healthy body, mind and spirit. In addition, I reasoned that if I only performed my daily intentions when I felt like it, I would be in danger of not making them a priority. I decided that as a corollary I needed a small general schedule, nothing too obsessive, that would encourage me to recall myself to purpose each day. The schedule would elevate these divine intentions above my natural inclination for early morning slothfulness. Sort of a monastic daily office; a reminder that I was not out here in the world merely to have a big fun holiday. I was on a sabbatical, for heaven's sake, a holy quest, to give undivided attention to making inner spiritual directions concrete, internalized and central to my daily life and decision making. Right next to my intentions I posted the following:

- **7 AM +/-** **wake up, turn on coffee, ease into the day (be careful of this!)**
- **7:30** **exercise**
- **8:15** **pray/meditate**
- **9:00** **eat? journal?**

Just that fast I ran into a mind absorbing dilemma. Exercising before food was a priority. The optimal time for prayer and meditation is when the body is limbered and relaxed. Then what? Was it better or easier to write in a journal when everything was still fresh in the mind from the quiet time? Or should I eat breakfast in order to keep to a healthy food schedule? Was it possible to do them together? Then there were the morning ablutions which my schedule did not seem to allow for at all.

Sadly, my good intentions were constantly assaulted by my natural inclinations which, for some reason, I felt that I should transcend. Of course, it did not occur to me that by trying to schedule my spiritual life, ego was taking over again. Once again I was allowing my preconceived ideas to be in the driver's seat, setting up how and when the inner voice speaks. But I get ahead of myself.

Camping life took on a rhythm of its own while I gradually adjusted to living on the road. I was chagrined to discover that my bio-rhythms changed as well. My natural self loved to wallow in the bed every morning with coffee and books, which I call easing into the day. In all honesty, for thirty years I found early morning rising and being alert quite biologically shocking.

I am one of those persons who come alive after sunset, content to leave the sunrises, beauteous as they are purported to be, to the morning people. I carried a fantasy through childrearing and fulltime working that one of the privileges and joys of being an empty nester was not having to waken on someone else's ungodly schedule. It didn't take me long to discover, however, that most campers are dedicated enthusiasts who arise early to cram as much activity as possible into their short vacation days. By 7 AM cheery voices shouted to each other over outdoor stoves as if the speakers were in their own kitchens. Everyday someone asked Honey if she had seen sneakers, screwdriver, billfold, or the baby's nook. In other words, life in the campground was a duplicate of daily life everywhere.

Compounding the insult was realizing that time, habit and peri-menopause had done their evil work. What had once been biologically shocking was now biologically inevitable. The first lightening of the windows over my bed ordained instant wakefulness. One would think that with all kinds of time I could keep to the simple discipline and schedule I had worked out.

On October 1st I wrote: "For some mysterious reason I did not write in this journal for over a week. I kept meaning to, then ignoring it. Why do I do this? Part of the reason may be that I am now writing an outline for a book on women's spirituality. The topic has grown out of the conversations I have had with women I've been meeting in the campgrounds this past month. In fact, those conversations are what have interfered with my daily office. I think they are sabotaging my purpose."

Oh right! The only *mysterious reason* I could find in all my writings was that I was thoroughly and completely involved in the life around me. Immersed in my new transient community, insatiably curious about the people I met I was caught up in the social kinetics at work. In other words, once again I faced my epiphanal truth: *everything is different but nothing is changed.* **It was just as easy to get distracted living in a van as it was at home.**

The woman directly across the road had been eyeing me every morning while I wrote in my journal. When I looked up and caught her eye, she waved, weakly, as if surprised that her arm could move on its own. That day I called out to her, inviting coffee and conversation. Curious, she was, about a woman traveling alone, no husband, no one to plug-in and set-up the campsite. She was not quite willing to believe that I was loving life's first solitude. Her words were softly spoken, but her eyes betrayed a drama of another sort playing out inside. I knew that I was about to become the holder of personal revelations.

They were packing up to leave, she said, cutting short their annual retreat on the Atlantic dunes. Her sister was dying, you see, consumed by the cancer that was not supposed to move this fast. Death and doctors had tricked them into believing that they had all the time in the world, at least another year. And so I closed my journal and we talked of sisters, and slumber parties; of parents too old to bear the burden, and children too young to understand; and of God and faith and ploughing on when your soul aches with sorrow. She squeezed my hand with shy gratitude, reluctantly said goodbye and left to pack, while I put away my writing and headed for the beach, determined to outwalk the gauzy ghosts her presence evoked.

Another day I met a woman whose desperate energy filled the laundry room. Quietly I looked around wondering where on earth I could sit to be out of the path of her frenetic pacing and compulsive folding. I took out my journal while my clothes washed themselves and put the date at the top of the page just as if I were going to write. Her hiccupping sobs tore out in savage bursts stopping my motions and tightening the muscles in my stomach. I looked up to see her clutching a piece of clothing, a tee shirt, in her hands and rubbing it across her wet cheeks and nose, inhaling sporadically. I was paralyzed, torn between the impulse to give aid and comfort and not having the slightest idea what to do.

"This is his! This is my boy's. His stuff shouldn't be mixed in with ours!" Her words brought on a fresh round of sobs when she buried her nose once again in the fabric. I knew she wasn't addressing me, but simply the humanity I represented. "He's only nineteen and they've sent him over there to Kuwait." Ah, my heart stutters. This was about wars and rumors of wars. This was the true primal scream of the mother whose young was ripped from within the walls of her protection and sacrificed on the altar of what we're being told is the collective good.

"This is his sock. It shouldn't be here." I didn't know what to say. I had never walked in her moccasins. Maybe my anonymity was the best I could offer, the uninvolved stranger who made no judgments. I silently closed my journal, knowing there would be no more writing that day as my head and heart wrestled with the meaning of violence and war, peace and love, and the letting-go of sons and daughters. If God did not require that of Jacob and Isaac, then why do we willingly give such power to the state? Another solitary walk on the beach was my only answer.

Each day brought forth a new conundrum. Yet each day I promised myself that I would definitely write in my journal. People, however, must have been meeting secretly and deciding who would approach me with hooks of compassion and empathy. I continued to hear about shaky marriages from people whose children were calling on them to help with childcare because of divorce and straitened economic circumstances. I listened to stories of people in recovery from addictions, disease, and bankruptcy. Nor were these the only distractions to my writing.

I never turned down being co-opted to make a fourth at bridge, or to come for supper. Frequently I was invited to join a group for dinner in town. When I stayed up late talking and drinking wine I knew my schedule would be useless the next day. In short, I was surrounded by real people whose real lives reflected and echoed every aspect of the work and world that I had left behind. The more I resolved to hold myself aloof from the pleasures and the pains of others so that I might follow the inner spiritual drive I so desired, the stronger was the seduction of being needed or wanted by the people around me.

The more I allowed people to occupy my time and thoughts, the less time I allotted for meditation, prayer and journaling. Yet how could it be a bad thing to spend time relating to people, and listening with compassion? Could it be that *good works and good intentions* separated me from the inner voice every bit as solidly as selfish pursuits and self-absorption? Armed with this question, I stepped off the train that was carrying me along the track of self-recrimination and into the centering place of meditative silence, seeking clarity and renewal of purpose.

I opened my journal and began the kind of writing that helps me bring order out of my own chaos. There is a kind of writing that flows from the inner self without editing or judging. I started with this question at the top of the page: *How can I stick to my purpose without being distracted?*

Reiterating my purpose, to live from the inside-out, I questioned the idea that all the people and all the stories were, in truth, distractions. The word *enhancers* appeared on the page. As I wrote, I began to understand that the stories and time spent with people were only distractions when they become *substitutes* for listening to the inner voice by co-opting my time and attention. If I were listening to the inner voice of God in a profoundly respectful way, waiting to discern in which direction to go, then those same distractions would be the enhancers of a life directed from the inside. People and books, wine and food are all distractions when they become the focus of my life, are the willful substitutions for being divinely led, or are the excuses used for ignoring the discipline of listening. When they are part of my response to the inner voice, however, they enhance my life with joyful meaning and purpose.

The fact that actions and interactions could be so inner directed that I would know where my energies and responsibilities could be of greatest value was a transforming thought. *And how*, I wrote in my journal, *am I going to learn to do this? Right across the page flowed the words: minute-by-minute-by-minute-by-minute ...*

The Outer Banks is a place of supreme oceanic environment. In October the days are perfect August days in New England. The low humidity of off-shore breezes keeps the sand from scorching and lulls the unwary into believing in endless summer. Shrimp boats lurk in the waters over the wrecks of more than 200 ships whose haunting hulks call to students of history and salvage experts alike.

I was content to merely walk the miles of white sandy shore, contemplating the fragility of living on a few yards of terra firma miles out in the Atlantic. When I stopped to talk to the fishermen casting for food in the roiling surf, they told me to keep my eyes on the clouds piling up on the horizon and the kelp washing up on shore. "Ma'm, you sure do wanna' be gone from here right soon after that. Could be hurricane's headed this way."

I automatically said to myself, "Let me know, God, when it's time to leave." I was having way too much fun to let it go. There were stories yet unheard, more swimming in the surf, and plenty of good southern food yet to eat. And, oh yes, listening, trusting and acting yet to experience.

Two days later I awoke on a Friday to bright sunshine, cloudless skies, very easy tides and minimal kelp. One more beautiful day in paradise. While walking along the edge of the tide, I knew that I should pack up and leave. The time had come.

My new friends teased me for being concerned about a hurricane. "Hey, even if one comes, we weather them every year. You're perfectly safe," assured the campground owner. "Stay a couple more days and you'll be headed north for your friend's wedding. Trust me," he exhorted with his hand in the air. Where had I heard that before?

His wife pitched in with, "We're having a shrimp party tonight. All you can eat. Come on, you don't want to miss it. Stay over the weekend. Look at that water. Nothing's on the way for at least another week. Tony's right. You're perfectly safe no matter which way it blows. You'll make the wedding even if we get a storm."

Tempted by their assurances and not wanting to make light of their greater experience, I almost gave in and said I would stay for the weekend. But something continued to niggle. Finally, I took the leap once again in trusting what I was hearing, packed up, said my fond goodbyes, took the ribbing and headed back to the mainland. By the time I drove a couple of hours, the rain was pounding the van and visibility was minimal. I called my daughter in Washington, D.C. and made quick plans to drive north and stay with her for the weekend.

That night while lying on the sleep sofa watching the late night news, I was stunned to see and hear that a hurricane had hit the Outer Banks that day. High winds smashed a barge into the bridge I had traversed that morning, completely cutting-off residents and tourists from leaving. It would be weeks before it could be repaired. The only other way to leave was the ferry at the southern tip of Ocracoke. Traffic backed up for miles as people were being turned away to await better weather and conditions. All the while, the reporter's face was unrecognizable from the unrelenting force of slanting rains. He signed off wondering where all those people would find shelter for the night.

I pulled the covers up around me in the relative peace and quiet of my daughter's living room, shivering with feelings and wonderment too huge to be contained. Drifting off murmuring my gratitude, my last conscious image was of sunny skies and warm welcoming water.

Chapter 9
Partners

The Falcon and I needed a period of adjustment to be comfortable companions before we could take to the open road with any degree of confidence or intimacy. As in any new relationship, we danced around for a time, testing whether or not we could commit to a longer-term affair. Becoming familiar with my partner's peculiarities demanded an enormous amount of my daily energy. The Falcon had some annoying habits I wondered if I could live with. First there were the pingy-pangy night sounds that were annoying when I wanted to relax. There was also a tendency to cranky motor sputtering when we had to get back on the road after a relaxing couple of days doing nothing. And what about the tendency to unexpectedly meander off the straight and narrow? I hated to be petty, but my grievances were constant reminders that healthy relationships require careful nurturing if they are going to last over time.

The Falcon embodied every physical, emotional and spiritual need of my new life. Home became condensed and stripped down to the absolute necessities for staying alive: a protected environment of safety and warmth. Staying in tune with its every idiosyncrasy so that I could determine when it needed something from me as opposed to merely expressing itself, was mandatory for my peace of mind.

Friends and family were fearful that I would be vulnerable on the road to the hideous violence that curses our culture. Interestingly, I never once worried about murder, rape or arson. Basically, my trust in the inner voice was so strong that I felt loved and protected in my wanderings and in the people I met. My greatest fear was that a Falcon tire would suddenly deflate on some lonely stretch of baking highway where I would have no access to services. Despite my bravado, I knew there was no way I could ever jack-up that camper and lift a huge heavy tire off its base. Not wanting to create the very issue that I most feared, I worked overtime at not thinking about or obsessing about the tires. A lot of good that did me.

Living from the inside of a nineteen foot camper after years of living in a rambling New England farm house was like moving from the mansion into the tool shed. All the necessary elements for getting the work done were in place, but the space and organization were restricted in placement and comfort. Like a boat, every item had to be tightened, bungeed or anchored firmly in its resting place before sailing down the highway. Grandma's incantation, "A place for everything and everything in its place," was not simply an aphorism, it was a necessity born of a gut-clenching truth if the Falcon and I were to travel safely together.

As eager as I was to simplify the accumulation of a lifetime of stuff, there were a few things I doubted I could be without for a whole year. The Falcon came equipped with a short countertop kitchen containing a tiny sink, a four-burner propane gas stove, and a built-in refrigerator about the size of the one my son took to college. There was no room on the minuscule counter for a microwave, TV or video cassette player.

Before I left the driveway, I faced the humbling self-knowledge that as spiritual as I might think myself, I did not quite trust that I could go a year without access to the worldly pursuits of topical news and renting a movie when boredom or loneliness inevitably took over. Not very lofty, I admit, but that was a time for bare bones truth. And microwaves make popcorn, steam vegetables, roast chicken and fish, and are fast sources of hot water, hot soup and reheating everything, especially when the weather is bad.

Eventually, I worked out a new system. A microwave oven fit perfectly on the closed top of the stove and could easily be strapped down while traveling. The open shelf above the frig was a snug fit for the VCR. And a very high-powered, *five- inch* portable TV was small enough to place on the top of the microwave when needed. As the living-room couch was only two feet or so away, viewing was very comfortable. When I sat on the couch my knees were in the kitchen. (My first viewing of *Dances with Wolves* was on that diminutive set. It lost something on a diminutive screen!)

Those new additions meant that I was committed to not using the gas stove inside the van. I packed a propane camping stove in the storage box to use outside, and somewhere in Florida I bought a portable gas grill as well. The best of all possible worlds: grilling and eating outdoors in great weather; popcorn and movies indoors anytime. I was set. Having absolutely no previous experience, I could only hope that I had made the right decisions. Whether or not it would work for a year was in the hands of the camping gods.

Storms and other inconveniences—

Fall is a time of hurricanes and unpredictable weather on the Atlantic seaboard. Naively ignoring twenty years of experience in New England, I did not prepare myself one iota for what to do when the rains slashed at the van and winds moved mountains of water. I had a rain poncho plus a cute matching bright blue hat and slicker, but no emergency equipment in case the electricity went off. I left the North Country in the sunshine, headed south into sunshine, and somehow expected that my little Falcon would literally weather every storm I met. Where was my head?

When the first storm hit the first week in Chincoteague, I awoke to the rocking of the van, the wind howling like Irish banshees, and thunder so loud it shocked the ground. When I raised the blinds, lightning lit the campground like mid-day so that for a second I could see water rapidly filling in the low spots. Taking a mental inventory, I was safe, snug and only slightly apprehensive. Then like a shock of electricity running through me, I remembered two things. I had not taken down the retractable awning on the side of the Falcon. And somewhere on the ground, possibly already covered with water, was the electrical connection from the Falcon to the electric hook-up box. To rescue either one might require my electrocution.

I shivered in the bed straining to hear if the thunder could be a bit farther off, if the lightning might not be coming so often. Damn! That awning cost me hundreds of dollars that I had agonized over spending. Praying for safety I threw on the rain poncho, stepped out into the deluge and hand over hand followed the cord from the van into the dark, terrifyingly aware that standing in three inches of water made me a lightning magnet.

I found the connection, blessedly not yet inundated, and safely looped it over a low-hanging branch. I dashed back to the van in misery seeing that the awning indeed had begun to torque in the wind. Its slim metal poles were not designed to anchor it in such a forceful deluge, but they could work as lightning rods. Now I not only stood in water, I was handling metal rods and trying desperately to manually retract the awning safely. Freezing with fear and soaked to the skin, I could think of nothing to do but to keep struggling until I finally got the awning rolled most of the way back into its aluminum holder.

Thankfully, I rushed back inside anxious to peel off my wet garments and realized that with the bed engulfing all the interior space, I had no place to shake off the water, undress and get rid of my wet gear. "OK, God," I said, "This wasn't part of the deal!" I shivered in the dark until I figured out a way to wiggle out of my wet things so I could crawl over the bed to reach a towel, find dry clothing and a flashlight. All the while I was talking out loud to the Sender of Storms seriously questioning my sanity. What in the name of all that was holy was I doing?

Snuggled down in my warm dry bed, I felt the darkness wrap itself around me like a gentle blanket while the Falcon protected me from all but the music of the rain hitting the roof. I could not close my eyes; I was too wired. Then I knew I was not just wired, I was energized.

Be still, the words came into my consciousness. *Be still and know*...I breathed those words deeply into my diaphragm and let the residual anxiety go as I breathed out. *What do I know?* I asked myself. And in the soft silence what I knew was that I was safe. I was warm. I had achieved something important. I did what needed doing. I set about a task so fearful and distasteful that everything in me wanted to hide from it. Though I was alone and afraid, I met the storm and did not allow it to overwhelm me. And the next time, I promised myself and all the Holy Angels as I fell asleep, I will be prepared. I will at least have a lantern to see in the dark. Meanwhile, the Falcon enfolded me in a resting place. Perhaps this would be more than a marriage of convenience.

Parking a recreational vehicle requires practice and expertise, neither of which I had when I started on my idealized journey. I remember that I drove the camper to a deserted parking lot one weekend before I left Massachusetts just to get the feel of backing it up and parking. Naturally, there was no comparison between that wimpy exercise and the reality of highways, parking lots, toll booths, gas stations and camping spots.

Of all of these, the worst for a woman alone is pulling into a camping site that requires backing in. Like every other institution, the camping world is hierarchical. The bigger, louder, longer the rig, the more space, room and respect it's given. Little guys, like my Falcon, took the sites that sometimes looked like they were designed for pop-ups or tents. Instead of being open and level, they can be down the twisty road, around trees with roots bumping-up in the middle, and squeezed in between kids, bushes and picnic tables. It became a game to see if I could find an available spot that either had an empty space behind with clearance between so I could pull through, or if I could find one on the end so I did not have to agonize over whether I was going to hit a tree or somebody's gear, rig or child. The trick was to park without too many awkward turns inching forward, turning the wheel, jerking backward, forward and backward, reminiscent of learning to parallel park. The actual learning was embarrassing enough; it was unbearable when the guys all come out to watch.

I loathe stereotyping, especially when it is seriously used in place of becoming acquainted with anything different from ourselves. Women are just as guilty of making generalizations about masculine behavior as men are about women. But I must say that 99.9 % of RV drivers are men. Occasionally you will see a woman taking a turn while her partner takes a break, but generally, it's a male thing. The same is true when pulling into camp. The division of labor is mostly traditional. *He* takes care of the outside: parking, hooking-up water and electricity, leveling the rig, arranging any outdoor equipment, hauling wood for campfires. *She*, meanwhile, takes care of the house: seeing to the kitchen, unhooking things that were tied down, testing appliances, setting out important personal items like family pictures and silk flowers, gathering the laundry for the laundromat. When the odd person comes along who is alone, *she* provides the evening's entertainment.

I circled around the campsite several times praying that the angle into my assigned space wasn't as critical as it appeared. My hands slipped in sweat on the steering wheel when I realized how close to the other sites my spot was. Would I ever get blasé about parking this thing? On the fourth go-around I said, "Oh, hell, you have to stop sometime. Give it a try."

I pulled past my site, stopped, then slowly backed up, desperately trying to use my side mirrors to check all the angles. I knew there was a picnic table somewhere back there, but I blanked on locating it. I stopped the Falcon and jumped out just to make sure I was not about to plow into anything. As I climbed back into the van, I noticed that a man in the camper next to where I was parking had come over to the tree line separating our sites. He folded his beefy arms over his chest, spread his legs and watched, clearly enjoying the show.

My face felt as hot as my hands. I looked out the front window and noticed that two more men had come to the edge of the road glancing at each other then flicking their heads in my direction wearing smirky smiles. My new neighbor, feeling it was time to lend a hand, stepped over the line and started motioning me from behind. This galvanized the other watchers into crossing the road and acting as point men in the front. With all three of them motioning, yelling "come on, come on, whoa, whoa" spinning their fingers in the air, telling me to turn, I felt like a pilot being semaphored to a jet-way.

By the time I climbed down, I was mortified to discover several clumps of interested campers watching the scene from the road. Thankfully, they retreated with friendly waves and cheers. My drama, however, was not quite finished.

All three of my rescuers approached with the typical campers' welcoming words and smiles, all the while checking out the Falcon, indiscreetly glancing in the windows. They did everything but kick the tires. Finally, one of the men couldn't stand it any longer and just had to ask. "Where's your old man?" Before I could answer, one of the others jumped in with, "Hey, if he's taking a nap or isn't feeling too good, we don't want to disturb him." Not to be left behind, the third chirped, "We could see you weren't too used to parking this thing. But it wasn't too bad." They all smiled hugely, for he might as well have added, "for a woman," because it surely hung in the air.

To my horror I felt a roseate stain suffuse my skin as I somewhat contritely confessed that the only 'old man' I had on this trip was the Falcon. The three slack jaws and incredulous faces made up for their inadvertent reminder of my single status. They shocked a laugh out of me that knocked my momentary lapse of mortification into the ether. They couldn't wait to get away. They started to back up all the while muttering things like:

"Well, whaddya know, all by herself."

"All the way from Massachusetts."

"Well, uh, glad to help out."

"The missus will want to have you over to supper."

"You need anything else, just let us know."

And finally: "There was a young lady came through here, on her way to California, wasn't she?"

"Yeah, yeah. But she was a young one." Silently I thanked him for the comparison.

"Had a job or something in California. Where did you say you were going?"

After several of these incidents, I took myself into a crowded mall parking lot and drove around until I found a spot where several large RV's were parked near the perimeter. I practiced for hours backing-in between vehicles until using mirrors and windows became comfortably automatic.

94

It's not that I minded help when I needed it. I simply did not want to attract any more attention than necessary. In all fairness to the men who helped me over the course of the year, they were always willing to lend a hand. And once over the idea that there was something strange about a woman their age camping across country alone, they were amazingly supportive and helpful. Invitations to dinner abounded, as much a part of the grace of hospitality that flows so freely in campgrounds as out of curiosity to hear the story of someone living life differently.

From the very beginning I struggled with holding the Falcon on a straight course. I made excuses. It was top-heavy by design. The road was uneven. The wind on the highway was unusually high. I was unused to its idiosyncrasies. It was natural to feel uneasy when first driving a vehicle that is totally foreign in size and shape. I just needed time and experience.

The day I drove the 17.6 miles of the Chesapeake Bay Bridge-Tunnel was overcast with the threat of rain. A state trooper was pulling RV's over to make sure all propane gas tanks were turned off. I did not know that propane tanks in tunnels were a no-no. More than ever, I was happy that I made the decision not to use my partner's. Trusting that all was copasetic, the Falcon and I entered one of the wonders of the world at the north end, passing over a high steel girder bridge that spanned a sea route. The wind buffeted the Falcon mercilessly forcing me to drive slowly in the right lane, hanging on with both fists and fighting to remember to breathe. The long stretch of trestled roadway between the entrance and the exit seemed interminable as the van swayed in the wind, trying to lead me off the road.

The visitor's center, where I had planned to stop for coffee while I gloried in seeing the Bay from this perspective, went right out of my vision. Stopping would mean starting again. It was better to keep going and get out of danger. The two-mile long tunnels at the south end which had been my biggest worry were beckoning refuges from fear and signaled that the end of the trip was near. Once off the bridge-tunnel, I was relieved and grateful for being physically whole and emotionally empowered and far more experienced testing the limits of my abilities to handle my vehicle.

Once again, the Falcon and I made it through a harrowing time together, cementing our relationship and trust. The nagging thought that the van shouldn't be that difficult to handle or that there might be something wrong got tucked away until one remarkable day in hot, steamy Florida.

Though I had no itinerary, I had always wanted to see the Florida Keys. In my daily listening for guidance to know where to go, I was heading farther and farther south. Buoyed by the news that my children and a friend would meet me for Christmas in South Carolina in a few weeks time, I was singing my way south. Life was good! The Falcon and I were getting along, I was excited about what I was learning, and my spiritual direction was saying Florida Keys! Glory!

It was late afternoon in northern Florida and the heat shimmered off the highway in dancing waves. I glanced at my gas tank, which was something I became compulsive about over time. Appalled at the amount of gas the Falcon drank, and how quickly, I did not want to add running out of fuel to my growing list of fearful experiences. Comfortable that there was enough gas to get us to a campsite I went back to my singing. As clear as a Buddhist bell a voice urgently said, *Get off the highway, now.* Startled I looked around. *Get off at the next exit. Check your tires.* I immediately tried to talk myself out of having heard a thing. My imagination was working overtime. I must have been daydreaming.

Again I heard, *Get off the highway now. Get off at the next exit.* Sure enough, an exit was fast coming up. Without more thought, I signaled and slowed down to exit where there was a gas station at the end of the ramp. I pulled in and started the pump, legs shaking. Feeling more than a little foolish, I asked a young mechanic if he would please check my tires. I did not trust my abilities to test them myself. He threw me a look of exasperation, but pulled a gauge out of his pocket and bent to the chore. He straightened up quickly and walked into the garage, leaving me to wonder if I was being brushed off. He soon returned with a man of indeterminate age, covered with grease, front teeth missing and an accent straight out of Appalachia. I was beginning to feel vulnerable and wary.

After checking the tires he said, "Lady, yor the kind I scrape up off the highway. Yor a death waitin' to happen." His words barely registered; they didn't make sense.

"Three of them tires got the right amount of air like they're supposed to. That there rear one's got 90 lbs. In this heat it sure is gonna blow. You couldn't last much longer out there on that road on a hot day like this." He looked at me accusingly, "Did you put air in them tires today?" I was not only speechless, I was confused.

"They're new tires. I haven't put any air in them since I left home," I stammered at him. "almost three months ago."

He shook his head. "Three months? You been drivin' on that tire for three months?" He stared at me in disbelief. "Yor one lucky lady."

He explained to me that new tires are over-inflated in order to mount them, then deflated to the correct poundage after they're in place. Obviously, someone forgot to deflate my fourth tire.

He shook his head and looked me right in the eye. "Lady, you either got an angel sittin' on yor shoulder or someone up there sure is lookin' out for you. Not a week goes by that we don't hafta' scrape someone like you off that highway." He waved away my thanks and offer of payment. "Wouldn't be right takin' money for savin' the life of someone with her own personal angel, now would it?" I watched him walk back into the mechanic's bay wanting to call out to him that angels came in all guises.

When I got back into the heavy southbound traffic of 95, I was shaky and slightly nauseated, imagining myself spread all over the road. Finding a campground and setting up camp was beyond my capabilities at the moment. At the next exit I drove my *partner* up to the first motel available that met all my criteria: pool, exercise room, room-service, full sized bathtub, a real bed and a huge TV. The Falcon and I needed a break from one another.

I wallowed. There is no other word for it. I wallowed. I wrapped myself in the sensate pleasures of cool waters, perfumed soaps, and service; lots and lots of being waited upon. Chilled wine for the bathtub with bubbles and good novel. Food that was intricately and delicately prepared by someone else just for me. All the while I was fizzing with the guilty pleasure of ignoring my main partner out in the parking lot. By the end of the evening, I was ready to take out my journal and record the sequence of the day, recalling myself to my purpose and intentions.

I could not ignore the memory of the day months before when trying to live from the inside out seemed unrealistically absurd and impossible. I was debating with myself that day whether or not my whole scheme was a self-deluding folly when I recalled the words that had rocked me months before, *When you are out in the world, my voice will be the only voice you hear.* It was with tearful humility that I heard that same voice this very day saying, *Get off the road now.* And thank you, God, that I took the spiritual voice seriously, that I put value on the inner voice and learned to *hear* it. What more proof did I need that I was on the right path, that I was on the right journey for me at this time?

Several miles down the highway I realized that something felt easier and different steering the Falcon. My partner must have done some soul-searching of its own while we were apart, for I was not struggling to keep the van from tugging off course. Hallelujah! Getting all four tires in sync had created a harmony between us that was freeing. We could ride down the open road with the wind at out backs joyfully and together. However, I could not remove the slight dread I still felt when I thought of our tire episode, wondering if we were truly over that issue, or if we would have to revisit the problem again.

Chapter 10
Co-creator with God

I played tag with the tide today
and danced along the sand.
I dared the sea to come and play;
yelled "catch me if you can!"

Poseidon raised his mighty head
and gave a thunderous roar.
But I was full of Self and glee
so tempted him for more.
Edisto Island, SC, November

While kicking down the beach on Edisto Island, South Carolina, I played a silly game with the incoming surf, childishly dodging around each patch of water while trying to keep my feet from being soaked. That night I started a poem: *I played tag with the tide today/ and danced along the sand./I dared the sea to come and play/cried "Catch me if you can."* In that moment I was every person who dances on the edge of nature's power, who has the temerity to believe that the universe exists at and for our pleasure. That we invite the unleashed power of the seas to play our little games is an illusory assumption that we are ever in control. What amazed me was not that I was spending time contemplating such philosophical themes, but that I would write a poem to express it.

On another occasion I sat on the dunes thinking about how trite is the concept that the older I get the less I know. Until, that is, one lives long enough to experience its truth. And sure enough, on the page the next day these words showed-up: *I don't know much, but this I know/ where sand meets sky the grasses grow.* There was definitely a poetry phenomenon springing forth. Why poetry, a device of self-expression foreign to me? Except for writing limericks and doggerel for special events, I was not known for being able to express myself in the concise spare language poetry requires. Yet for some unexplained reason, I needed to express myself in that lyrical style. It wasn't until I hauled out the watercolors that I really began to worry, or more concisely, pay attention.

I'm the one who flunked art in kindergarten. Cutting and pasting were a nightmare; drawing was a skill beyond my scope. I envied anyone who could conjure form and substance from colorful media and translate them onto canvas and paper. Early on, I learned that the visual arts were off my talent chart. Yet here I was with a compulsion to paint that was visceral. I simply had to do it.

I had to try to capture the brilliant colors of an evening sun slipping into the purple waters off the Florida Keys. I yearned to record the beckoning green shade of Carolina live-oaks draped in their luminous, pearly hanging-moss. I felt compelled to keep a record of pellucid underwater plants whose colors swirled in the shallows of vivid turquoise bays. And always, always, everyday to try one more time to translate onto paper the immediacy of the water. I felt that I was waking-up to the infinite variety and beauty of the earth. As strange as it sounds, I felt that I was *seeing* the world for the first time.

Trying to paint what I saw turned me upside down. Leaves were not green as I had always assumed in my enjoyment of spring and summer landscapes. Leaf greens are mixed with the subtle shadings of a million other colors so that no two of any kind are alike. And the same is true of the bark of trees. They were not brown as I had always blithely thought. Well, maybe a little brown, but a lot black and gray with bits of white or green in the knots and hollows. Try to paint the sky. By the time you dab a bit of the proper paint onto the brush, the density and complexity of the overlay of color has shifted into a wholly new configuration of form and depth. Where had I been all my life that I did not notice that life in all its forms was in the rich detail of distinction?

All that fall I gloried in the creative process with a freedom wholly new and deeply satisfying. There was no audience, no one to see or to hear or to read, or to judge, except the Holy Spirit and me. What was even more amazing was that the more creative I allowed myself to be the more I tended to the disciplined details of my intentional life. The daily decisions about budgeting, food, maintenance, and scheduling became less arduous and onerous. Far from preventing me from attending to the important details of daily living, deliberate creativity was a wellspring out of which flowed the energy and discernment to achieve external tasks with equanimity and relaxation. Why had I not learned of this years ago?

The answer, I think, goes beyond priorities and choices. It goes to *values*. Personally, I value art in all its manifestations as one of the highest forms of human endeavor. Art has the capacity to lift us out of our everydayness, to transcend our lives, to inspire us to aim for higher good, or to portray our flawed nature to ourselves. Art pushes the boundaries of complacency and challenges us to find the extraordinary in the ordinary. I was no stranger to art; I put a high value on it. Since childhood I have been transported, awed, by the gifts of the talented translators among us.

That was the point. I put a high value on Art, the kind that Artists create, and the kind I was willing to take time out of my busy to life to pay for and to pay attention to, hoping for that momentary connection which comes with the 'ah-ha' I anticipated receiving. My attempts at poetry, painting and music were never going to be in that league. Nor was it important that they should. What I was learning to do was to *put value on my own creativity without judgment.*

During the UN Decade of Women Conference in Nairobi, several of us from disparate backgrounds met for dinner at an outdoor restaurant to discuss our various thoughts and ideas about the conference. When the meal was over and all the intellectual and ideological ideas wound down, there was an easing of our minds into the elastic awareness that the time had come for which we were truly intended.

We sat in the semi-darkness and spoke quietly of our lives, our families, and our dreams. Without the constraints of performance expectations, we opened up our hearts. We were Egyptian, American, sub-Saharan African, and European. We were Catholic, Protestant, Muslim and Agnostic. Yet when we dug deep beneath those labels, we were simply women speaking eloquently together about what women everywhere value and support: healthy families, education for the children, a chance to earn a sufficient living, and a peaceful world in which to prosper.

"This is what we call creativity," the African woman told us. Those of us from the North asked her to explain.

"In our tribal life, we believe that the sole purpose for our being here on earth is to create. The Spirit that gave us the land wants us to work to meet our needs. But our true work is to create." Intrigued, I asked her to tell us what this meant in terms of everyday life.

"Unlike industrialized cultures," she said, "where people are rewarded for working most hours of the week away from family, which leaves only a spare time for what you call leisure or the pursuit of artistic expression, we believe in the opposite. Work is simply to sustain the body and the community, which is done with minimal time and effort. The majority of time each day is spent passing along the creative aspects of life to the young."

She then described how the elders of the village teach story-telling, passing along tribal creation and life-sustaining myths; they pass along indigenous secrets of dye-making, painting and weaving, of musical instruments, singing and dancing, of herbs and healing rituals. In this way, everyone contributes to the creative process of collective life. Everyone is perceived as being not only part of the *created*, but also as part of the *creative*.

Was this a bit of indigenous wisdom being awakened in me all these years later as part of the evolution of aging? Did it come from some atavistic genetic memory that it was now my turn to "pass it along?" Perhaps. All I knew that fall by the sea was that I was hungry to create, and that the very process of creating was freeing me in some indefinable way to absorb a different set of values and priorities. What it did was shepherd me toward the understanding that creativity is part of our humanness, given to all of us. My watercolors will never hang on anybody's wall nor will my poetry take any literary prize. But that was not their purpose. Their purpose was to *free me* from the confines of narrow judgment and to explore the limitless possibilities life holds.

And so it was as autumn wound down that I continued to paint, and to write in my journal, and to surprise myself with the occasional poem. The night winds turned colder as December loomed on the calendar prompting me to begin my daily asking in earnest. *When should I leave here?* And the answer seemed to be, *not yet.*

It was no hardship to trust that I needed to stay longer as I moved from Key Largo down to Bahia Honda State Park. I made forays to the other Keys to explore their beaches, loving the Caribbean climate, praying that the snakes and alligators would not come out to play. I embraced the incongruity of wearing shorts and bathing suits while humming holiday carols in stores decorated with angels and shepherds.

Christmas shopping in Key West with the retired couple parked across the road from me proved to be a day of mixed delights. The husband was a retired engineer. His wife, desperate for company, was having some struggles adjusting to full-time living in her thirty-two foot home. They were excited to show me the sights of the most famous part of the Florida Keys. Not wanting to spend money on food, they packed a lunch and off we went to the very tip end of Key West, Zachary Taylor Park. It was a gorgeous day, clear, sunny, not too hot with a mild breeze and unending sapphire water. When my host kept up a running monologue on the horrors of the weird people we would be exposed to when we left the natural beauty of the park, I started to worry.

Then we hit Duval Street, the main part of town, made famous in story and song. Shops, crowds of people, holiday music wafting from several directions, people humming and grooving to the sounds. I immediately headed for the sidewalk art displays out of curiosity for anything indigenous to the culture of the Keys. I only wanted to find one exotic kite for my son to fly on his beach in northern Massachusetts; they insisted that we hit every T-shirt shop in town. I was entranced by the atmosphere, the rich variety of people: bikers, suburbanites, honeymooners of several orientations, families, and every conceivable color on the earth. My host kept pointing out the *weirdoes* we women were to beware. I got more and more uptight at his uptightness. When it was time to eat another meal, things came to a head.

I held out for something touristy like Jimmy Buffet's Margaritaville, lookin' for that peripatetic shaker of salt. In truth, until that moment I had no strong need to neither eat in the famous restaurant nor drink a margarita. But I stood on the sidewalk in front of the place and declared my intention as though I were starving and this was manna. They were horrified. They thought Wendy's was the better choice, cheaper and not so patronized by, you know, *strange folk.* By that time, I would have given everything I owned to be free of their constraints. I suggested that we split up and meet later, but that idea collided with their adamant insistence that I needed their protection. I felt myself regressing to my thirteen-year-old self getting ready to pitch a fit because my parents were wet-blanketing my fun. Surely there was a more *creative* way to handle my feelings now.

Being creative sometimes means compromising. I still laugh when I see us that late afternoon. They came along to stare at me. While I crunched on deep-fried conch rings and defiantly sipped a frosty margarita, they refused to buy even a coke or water. Later I trailed after them and drank pedestrian coffee trying not to look appalled when they went back for the sixth and seventh times at Wendy's Super Bar.

Our differences evaporated on the pier at sunset, borne away on the plaintive sounds of the highland piper and the carnival antics of hoop-jumping cats, palm readers, psychics, sword swallower, and on and on. What energy! What fun! I watched the small smiles on my cohorts' faces, and the day fell into perspective. They were observers; I was a participant. They cerebrate before acting; I act then cerebrate. Heaven knows we need both skills, plus the discernment to know when each is appropriate and how to reconcile these opposites.

Like a flash it hit me. How like my marriage this insight was. He was the observer, I was the participator and over time we did not learn how to meld our differences. Even with this new understanding and lessening of resentment, I missed, in those moments, being with someone who could enter into life's experience with the same off-beat wacky fun the whole gestalt elicited in me.

When the sea swallowed the sun in one dramatic gulp, the pier revelers drifted off as night swiftly obliterated the daytime warmth, reminding us that winter was just over the horizon. The time for me to head north for a Hilton Head Christmas with my kids was nearing. I yearned for it to come soon. Suddenly, I had enough of strangers and the superficial politeness that accompanies getting acquainted. I longed for the company of those with whom I do not have to explain myself nor define my terms, nor tip-toe around the comfortably familiar. I missed the intimacy of knowing and being known. It must be time to move on.

Not yet, not yet, the voice inside insisted. I sat in the quiet of the Falcon while slanting rains pounded onto the land, the last fury of hurricanes from the south. *Read your journals,* came the message from within. The pilings on the pier near my campsite were almost obliterated by the storm. I could vaguely make out the tall piling where the old white pelican staked out his claim near the spot where fishermen cleaned their catches. *Where did he go in this weather?* I wondered, putting off my inner assignment. And where were all his little competitors, the terns and the gulls?

There seemed to be something else that I needed to pay attention to, something else that I needed to know or understand before I could move on. I read over the parts in my journal about creativity until I stopped at the thought that I am not only part of the *created,* I am also part of the *creative.* The more I read those words, the greater my recognition that this was the locus of what was teasing my brain.

Creativity, I thought, *was the art and the act of transforming anything into something of greater value.* Words into poetry; dyes into paintings; notes into song; pain into wholeness; sperm and egg into a child. In that sense, it is the human activity that most mirrors God the Creator. Harkening back to my journal where I wrote about women being particularly adaptable to the flow of the changes of tides and seasons, I had hinted at the feminine form as a holder of life, a nurturer and sustainer. Surely those are divine attributes.

The Christmas carols hummed so blithely while shopping returned to remind me of Mary, the archetypal mother. In my protestant world, we did not give Mary much room or recognition except in the stories of Christmas and Easter. Yet it hit me that together with the Creator, she gave birth to the Universal Child. Therefore, do not all women everywhere share in this sacred connection? Mary the Mother was *co-creator* with God to bring forth new life. Was it possible, then, that when we create we all become *co-creators* with God? The very act of creating anything: children, loving relationships, communities, healing, science, satisfying work, art, music, dance, storytelling, yes, even my poetry and watercolors, transforms our little lives onto the sacred stage where we dance in the universe with God. The African woman on that soft summer night in Nairobi had spoken an eternal truth. *Our real work in this life and in this world is to create.* And it is given to all of us; it is in our genes.

That was the lesson I had to learn. That was the truth I needed to know before I could continue on my journey. Those were the words I had unknowingly been hanging out to hear. My real work was not behind me; it was still ahead and would be until the end. Living from the inside out means being in the Godlike flow of bringing forth new life. This work is ageless.

The final few weeks of autumn, before the winter solstice, has historically been a time of introspection. Advent is the time when we are encouraged to look back at the year and reflect on what is past, to look at what we would do differently, to seek solace and forgiveness for those we have wronged, and to cleanse ourselves from the inside in preparation to receive the birth of God's and our infant newness and vulnerability.

I prepared myself for a leisurely reflective trip northward through the central part of Florida, skirting the exotic vastness of the Everglades. Driving through the citrus groves I was surprised by the number of western-style ranches. The interior lakes called to me, so blessedly peaceful after living so long at the capricious mercy of the season by the sea.

I traveled only as far each day as I felt led. I spent the remainder of the day walking through the parklands while consciously attempting to assess, take stock of the richness of the delicious variety of experiences of the last three months. Wondering, of course, for the thousandth time if what I was doing was smart for someone my age and stage of life. As if honoring my spiritual intention for retreat, no one approached me in the campgrounds that last week before I met my family, until the last night.

Naturally, because I had been wavering about being a little old to be living this way and wondering if I wouldn't be better off going home and earning a living, I got invited to supper by octogenarians.

The evenings farther north had grown nippy, so we ate inside their motor home. Like me, they were headed north to spend Christmas with family. Gracious, charming and southern, they fed me the lightest biscuits and the most exquisite chicken next to green beans cooked with ham with homemade pickled beets on the side. For dessert she had made a pecan pie that was so balanced in its flavors that when I forked it into my mouth I wanted to weep. This was the food of my childhood, of church suppers and grandma's house, of my mother's table and country inns. The conversation roamed the galaxy of families, life's experiences, quiet gentle humor at growing older and fierce opinions of war and peace and politicians.

The evening ended with their asking if we could pray our goodbyes together. In the atmosphere of shared lives this request served the content of our time together very well. So we linked hands around their tiny dinette and each of us spoke from our hearts the words we needed to pray. Each one blessed the others for their lives, giving thanks for the journey, praying for peace in our world. As I went out the door he patted me on the shoulder, eyes sparkling, "Never doubt that you have a rich long journey ahead of you. You are just getting started, young woman!"

I walked out into the blackness of the night and feasted on the stars, so brilliant in those places where there are no lights. I wondered if there truly were angels, those heavenly messengers who bring us the word. I had just been told by an 85 year-young man that my worries about age are relative, and that the journey is always ahead. Grateful in so many ways to be *here*, I hugged this Advent time to my heart, a gifted time to digest all the sights and sounds of world and soul I had experienced in so short a time.

The people, the stories, the *listening* that paid off in so many ways, the patterns of sand and life all spread before me like bright rings of gems on my fingers. The funny adjustments to living in a camper, the ease of being on the road, and the discovery of so much beauty in the world fulfilled my daily hours in ways I could not have conceived of before this trip. Finding freedom in being myself, waking up to the stultifying encumbrances of judgment and preconceived ideas, discovering that what distracts can also enhance, and feasting freely on creativity fed my spirit beyond what I had known was possible. I wanted to kick up my heels, share my song with the world. Instead, I quietly walked home in the enfolding darkness under the stars praying that all people everywhere could have the chance to reevaluate their lives from the inner core where the self meets the divine.

Whatever was in store on the next stage of my journey, I was an excited bundle of anticipation wanting only to savor in every way the time with David, Darrah and Steven. The mother part of me needed the touch, the teasing, the assurance that all was well with them. Or, maybe I needed the assurance that all was well with me away from them. There would be time later, on the next phase of my journey, to wrestle with exactly how I could turn my life into one of living to create.

Book III

Winter:
Texas

Chapter 11
Setting the Stage

We would rather be ruined than changed;
We would rather die in our dread
Than climb the cross of the moment
And let our illusions die.
W.H.Auden[8]

Christmas is all about relationships, the ones we love, the ones we struggle with, the ones we tolerate, and the ones we wish we had. As far as I can figure out, the ones we love and the ones we wish we had are far and away the sources of our greatest angst. The others, we know more or less what to expect. But attachment to family members and those who are unavailable cause some of our greatest emotional upheaval. Sometimes they are the same. "God put us in families," someone once said, "knowing that if we could figure it out and get along there, we could get along with people anywhere." I left Hilton Head satisfied that my three offspring were well on their individual ways to figuring it out and getting along. I wasn't so sure about myself. Not only were my preconceived ideas under attack, but so were my illusions.

The holiday was a test of sorts, different from our years of well-loved fireside traditions, proving that no matter where we landed we were yet a close and loving family.

We walked beaches, swam in outdoor heated pools, played billiards at the local sports bar. Our tree was festooned with nature's shells hung beautifully next to the shiny colors of packaged bows and bits and pieces of smooth sea glass tumbled in the surf. All transitory and disposable, not at all like the ornaments stored at home, lovingly collected over time to be brought out each year with anticipation and joy. Awkwardly wrapped packages that withstood traveling in duffle bags filled up the space underneath the tree giving the guys excuses to hector, tease, or defend their offerings.

"Hey, Steve! Wrapped those packages yourself, did you? Like the dinky bow work!"

"Yeah, well, at least I took the time to buy my stuff. Look at yours! Mom! Didn't you teach Dave anything? How could he think using grocery sacks wrong-side-out was Christmas paper?"

Brothers laughingly taunted each other, and I noticed how seamlessly they included their sister's fiancé in their antics. Their petite five-foot-one sister still hurried to keep up with the six-foot-one guys in every way. Some things never changed, I pondered in my heart with fierce maternal pride.

Their roots in themselves and each other were strong. They were all three testing their wings in dynamic ways with careers that satisfied. They were all three managing their lives living on their own without parental support. If they were having bumps in the road of relationships, then what was I to say? The divorce was a legacy that weighed heavily on my mind that Christmastide as I observed the fallout in my adult children.

There was one other person present at out family festival. He was a close friend of mine, a younger man who had been a constant support during the last year while I prepared myself for my sabbatical. Richie's humor and spirit were a healing balm to my soul as I emerged from the foggy cocoon of a prolonged divorce. I had missed him sorely since we said goodbye in September. As we spent time together that Christmas, reconnecting so effortlessly, I began to question what I wanted out of the relationship. Or, more accurately, I put undue pressure on a fragile friendship by wondering out loud what I wanted out of any relationship; or, indeed, if I wanted a relationship. My ambivalent soul-searching unfortunately threatened the easy feelings between us, as he so rightly pointed out that I was the one who left, who chose to say goodbye. I woke up to the subliminal illusions swimming underground in my psyche that I would only be complete when I found a life-partner. Unconsciously, I had been trying to fit Richie into that role. Disillusioned by my own vulnerable neediness and his total inappropriateness for a lifetime position, I sadly waved him off. Letting go of illusions is not only painful, it leaves an empty space in the inner landscape where unfulfilled expectations once resided.

My poor kids. What a role model! I wasn't any older than they in some respects.

Like them, I was wondering who I was and what I would need in a permanent relationship. Unlike them, I was in my fifties; they were in their twenties. I should have known that God wouldn't let a teaching opportunity like that go by. In the way of the divine comedy there were months down the road when I would have many chances to practice.

The air condition unit sat atop the Falcon like a stetson on a cowboy. Its pristine white crown towered over us lesser mortals on the ground. Unfortunately those extra inches got us in trouble as we parked in Fernandina Beach State Park, Florida the first night back on the road.

All day I rode the old roller coaster of emotions. One minute I was crying over leaving all I hold dear and familiar, and the next I was euphoric over the exciting bubble of lightness and freedom that came with knowing that I was finally heading out—away—on my own. I would not be seeing any of my children until next summer when my daughter, Darrah, made tentative plans to meet me in August at my parents' home in Indiana. That was nine whole months away!

Driving offered hours of uninterrupted reflection on where I had been, the people in my life, the nature of human relations. The first four months taught me that I could survive quite well on my own. Our Christmas together reassured me that my family did not feel abandoned. Our ties of love and generosity were strong enough to endure despite their father's choice of another family, and their mother's unorthodox journey into her own future.

Feeling good, feeling strong, I bounced in my seat while I sang out my promises to my own spiritual and emotional needs. My journey was more important to complete than trying to satisfy the emotional needs of another man simply to have the security of him in my life.

Whoosh. The center of my body literally dropped into a peaceful place when I could say out loud, for the first time in my life, that it was really okay for me to have needs and to meet them. I wasn't only getting older, I was really getting better! I tooted the horn and waved my fist. And all the horns in Florida answered me back!

I had landed myself in the middle of a caravan of alligators. Alligators were on hoods, windows, even waving eerily from antennae. The guys in the car to my left honked and waved their fists at me in imitation of what I had been doing minutes before. The alligator-hatted guy on my right leaned out his window, waving his fist and yelling something at me that sounded like "Go 'Gators!"

It was just my luck that when I reached a pivotal point in the development of individuated feminine autonomy, I was surrounded by the testosterone madness of hundreds of fans going to the 'Gator Bowl. Like fleas on a skillet they were hopping all over the place. All the motels were filled, restaurant parking lots were crowded, and getting gas meant a wait in a long line of hyper post-adolescents who were openly carousing. I couldn't help but laugh at some of their antics, but it was time to get off the road.

Alas, even that decision was not without its problems. The campground was packed, but there was a spot in one of that typical down-that-away-around-the-cypress-find-a-table-and-stake-your-claim sort of place.

"Oh yes, the ranger will come by to collect later. We're awfully busy. It's the Gator Bowl, you know?" When I showed the woman my ID and registration and she saw my last name, her eyes lit up. This was a common occurrence in Florida. *Here it comes*, I thought.

"Shula? Would you be any relation to Don, the Dolphin's coach?" I gave her my stock answer. "It's not my family." This usually shuts them up. This time it didn't. She went right over my head. "Gosh, you must love football. It's the Gator Bowl, you know. Are you going? You must love football, being a Shula and all."

"Not much," I mumbled trying to block out the rush of memories of my youngest son sitting in front of the TV wrapped in his Dolphin jacket for luck. She looked at my license.

"Well, you must be a yankee cousin." She damned with faint something or other, as if that explained everything. Maybe it did.

My earlier euphoria evaporated leaving me depleted, testy and just plain anxious to get hooked up and settled down. I had some heavy listening to do if I were to know where to go next. I needed peace.

My campsite naturally was between two Gator Bowl parties. When I tried to whip the Falcon around so that our backs were to the road, I managed to crunch the air conditioner beneath a huge hanging limb that would never lose an argument with puny plastic.

I climbed to the roof to survey the damage knowing that the tree was protected from the likes of me and my kind. Sure enough, the limb had crunched part of the plastic cover. I just sat down on that roof and contemplated my future. I figured that was as good a spot as any to sit quietly above all the bustle below and pray for peace, guidance and slip in a request that the AC damage was affordable. Fortunately, people who ran around with alligators on their heads didn't seem to notice anything amiss with a mature woman sitting on the top of her camper contemplating the world.

What came out of that quiet time were three things. I needed to tape the plastic top until I could replace it. I should immediately head west toward the gulf area. I needed to get off the road for the New Year's weekend and stay in a hotel because of the weather. All of this was fascinating because I did not know that 1) the plastic top was a separate piece that was replaceable; 2) following the curve of the water around the gulf had not previously occurred to me; and 3) getting off the highway over the New Years made safety sense, but the weather was perfect. Why not camp and save my money?

Remembering the tires and the hurricanes, I renewed my vow to follow the inner direction, to trust it and to act on it. After all, what did

I have to lose? I was truly on an adventure, why cobble it up with too much cerebrating. Tomorrow I would head west somewhere on the gulf coast. But where?

The day progressively worsened as the temperature dropped when fog and clouds replaced the sun. I spared a fleeting thought for the poor souls locked in an alligator stadium somewhere as I left the super highway to meander southwest toward the Gulf of Mexico. The map open on the floor next to me showed lots of little green pine trees, marking state parks dotting the route I was taking. But the weather was too iffy to contemplate stopping. It was eerie how accurate my inner voice was about the weather. So I persisted in driving long after my agreed upon time to stop.

Early on I learned that I needed to find a campground by late afternoon to ensure there was a vacancy, and to give me plenty of down time to move my body after hours of riding. I liked to get off the road by 4:30. On that December 30th, however, I just kept going. Nothing appealed or tugged at me to stop until I reached Route 98 and the sapphire waters of the Gulf. Miraculously, the fog and clouds lifted as the late afternoon sun, thin and watery, pulled me toward the west. I was entranced by the white sugar beaches at the side of a road that graciously wended its way along the contours of the land. I had the road to myself for long hypnotic stretches during which I could fantasize about what it would be like to live in such lush surroundings. Would people here accept a gypsy yankee divorcee of indeterminate future?

The indeterminate sun decided to call it a day just as the sign for Panama City loomed ahead. It was definitely time to follow my spiritual voice and get off the road for the holiday weekend. A hotel in Panama City with restaurant, music, people and a pool sounded about right. At that moment all I wanted was to stop driving and stretch. I wanted to curl up in a warm and protected place to contemplate the Christmas Past and how far I had to go in terms of *relationships* and *reconciliation.* I had no premonition of how stretching the weekend would be, nor how it would be the opening act for the main events to come over the winter. Nor how it would set the stage for the places I would go, the people I would meet, and the decisions I would carry.

By wondrous luck or timing, I found a new hotel on the beach with affordable off-season rates. If I felt a pang of remorse leaving the Falcon alone on a windy parking-lot so soon after we had gotten back into the rhythm of our symbiotic friendship, it didn't last long. Trying not to think that Hilton Head had spoiled me for the contemplative camping life, I turned my back on the van. Head down against the stinging wind and pulling my jacket tightly around me, I headed into the ease of pampered living.

I noticed the young men right away. They sat in a group around a table full of empty plates and long tall glasses. They were muscular, fit, and had short haircuts. One even sported a silky white scarf wrapped around his neck, tails hanging. They were brash in an inoffensive way, cocky and terribly, terribly young.

"Hey everybody! We're gonna' kick Saddam's ass." Their broad laughter brought them indulgent looks from the patrons, and knowing head shakes from several of the older men. I recognized them as well. I had seen their counterparts twenty years ago during the Vietnam War at several air force bases near where we had lived in Arizona and Alaska. They were definitely military and probably pilots. Perhaps even helicopter pilots like the men I had talked to at Elmendorf in Alaska. They wore scarves, too.

Those young men were pumped. They were on their last leave before deploying to Kuwait and Iraq. Their enthusiasm for combat was heartrending. I had to turn away, tears burning, as I wondered how many of them would return and in what condition. Even as I offered up a prayer asking for forgiveness for our willingness to sacrifice our young, I could not help but be drawn to the sheer joy they exuded despite their innocence of the horror of death and destruction. The paradox weighed me down. A man nearby smiled in sympathy as if he knew what I was feeling.

Eventually, I sat and talked to people, provoking a lively discussion with the southern contingent about women traveling alone. Was I an

117

'uppity woman?' I could not answer their question. I was reticent to admit in that festive company that I was on a spiritual journey exploring life from the inside out. *Is that uppity?* I wondered. Or should I be more of a proselytizer for the spiritual life. Was I in that place at that time to tell people about the inward journey? Was I abdicating some kind of missionary opportunity in the middle of the restaurant lounge to talk about internal peace with party-goers on the eve of war? Finally, the man I had seen earlier wandered over and introduced himself. The talk flowed easily and effortlessly between us. Sam was in charge of the young fliers at the rowdy table. I had no problem telling him about my quest.

Sam and I spent hours talking that weekend as the ebb and flow of New Year's celebrations brought us into contact. He was a veteran of combat experience, a career military man who had lost his illusions in Vietnam. He knew war for what it was, and he was agonizing over what these young men under his command were going to experience. And, I think, he was tormented for the commands he might have to give.

Sam gifted me with a glimpse into the soul of a warrior. Here was a man who took no delight in fighting or in the death of enemies.

"Look at them," he said to me, motioning toward his men with his head. "There's no talking to them. They're convinced they're invincible." He sadly laughed. "Just where I was twenty years ago. Poor buggers."

"But they have the advantage of your experience," I quietly offered.

He tore a piece off a book of matches and tossed it across the table. "Right. They have a man who dimmed his soul picking up bloodied bodies of kids just like them in rice paddies. Hell, *I* was just like them. We all were. Now I'm tired of sending kids out there, even when I know we need to go."

I did not know what to say. He looked at me and smiled as he sat back. "Some party conversation, huh? "

"Why do you stay in? Surely you have your twenty years by now?" I asked.

He leaned forward again, his eyes intent on mine. "Do you know your New Testament?"

I nodded dumbly not knowing what to expect. We had not discussed religion.

"There's a place where Jesus is being abandoned by his followers. He had finally gone too far for many of them. When he looks up he sees Peter standing there and asks him, 'What, are you still here?' And Peter says..."

"—where else would I go?" I softly finished the line. Sam sat back and just stared at me.

"Yeah. Where else would I go." He looked down at his hands and back up. "I have a son. He's fifteen. All his life his dad has been in the military. All his life he's heard his dad tell him he's in the military because the military needs guys that know the score and to make sure kids like him won't have to fight. He knows there is no glory in what we do, but sometimes it's necessary. I made a vow to protect and that takes precedence over any of my own personal questions and feelings. I promised." He shook his head. "This is where I have to be." His voice trailed off. "Yeah, where else would I go?"

My eyes filled with tears and he leaned over and took my hand. "Hey, I'm sorry to be such a drag." I started to protest but he shushed me. "No...no...listen to me. This weekend is hard for me. I brought those guys down here to blow off some of their steam before we deploy. Watching them gives me great pleasure and deep sadness at the same time. But," he took my other hand, "meeting you and being able to talk on this level, well...I can't say what a gift it's been. Doesn't happen too often. In fact," he laughed, "this is the first time."

Sam had matured beyond the mythic promises of war as glory, but not beyond the promises of judicious necessity. His world had carried him well past the happy innocence of his men. His eyes carried the message of a thousand years of knowledge that most of us, because of him, will never have to know. Yet he was choosing to take that journey again not knowing how the actions of another war might damage his soul. War was his job. He had "...promises to keep, and miles to go..."

Our talks were mutual, for he seemed as eager to have a glimpse into my soul as I was honored to see into his. He gave me words of encouragement, attentive silence and respectful questioning. For a brief time that weekend, I experienced the joy of knowing and being known, of a mutually supportive intimacy that came with no squandered neediness to be anything other than who we were in that moment. We wrestled only briefly with staying in touch. Then we said our goodbyes well. He asked me where I was going next and I replied, "Where the wind of God blows me." We hugged tightly and he whispered, "Me, too." He rounded up his crew while I headed back out to the Falcon.

The Falcon and I sat for a long time in that deserted parking lot, emptied of the hundreds of cars jammed in over the past two days. Here and there were bits of gaudy cardboard hats and the smashed remains of crepe paper horns. There was just me and the whole US of A before me and I hadn't spent one minute of the weekend praying about where I was supposed to be heading.

As I sat there on that cold blustery day contemplating the last week, I knew that my prayers must start with "Thank you, God, for all the lessons of this life…" Although I felt strongly about my focus on the inner voice, I knew that the gentle warrior gave me two powerful gifts. He showed me what a man looks like who is available and puts value on me. And he brought my attention out of the personal and onto the larger stage of a world desperate for healthy, loving integration. He made the threat of war real and the urgency of prayer personal and mandatory. As important as my journey was to me, it was only a part of the larger world. Our time together felt like a healing gestalt. "Go with God" I said out loud, and knew that I was saying it to us both.

Chapter 12
Interlude: Where Do I Go from Here?

Gray day—cold and VERY winter like—drove through Florida to Mobile to Baton Rouge. Stayed in a KOA (Kampground of America) ugh! Never again if I can avoid it.
 Journal: Louisiana, January

Winter weather made me cranky. Icy winds and threatening skies belonged far to the north, not where I was in Louisiana, land of bayous, shrimp and Cajun music. I was also cranky because I thought I might be going to New Orleans to eat beignets and listen to jazz. I also strained in lookout for the item on my list of places I must see this year. Lake of the Ozarks ought to be in Arkansas as well. But no, I could not find it on the map. Maybe, once again, I was deluding myself about this mysterious place. I felt so sure about it before I left home.

Yearning into my stillness, I heard not a word prompting me into the deep Acadian woods and rivers of Louisiana. Darn, keeping my promise to stay in tune with inner spiritual direction was supposed to be fun, fruitful and divinely inspired, not this gray, foggy heaviness that mirrored the winter chill. Furthermore, as the day progressed, the weather not only worsened, there were no campgrounds beckoning to me, either. Even more provoking was the temptation to stop in a motel again, which wasn't fiscally feasible. Spoiled by Christmas vacation and the Panama City hotel, I was in danger of becoming effete, afraid to rough it even the tiniest bit. I reminisced with painful longing about the warm beautiful days of autumn which I arrogantly assumed would be mine for the year. By the time it was late afternoon, I stopped finally at a private campground.

Campground is a generic term for a site to park your camper, pitch your tent, or unhitch your trailer. There are categories of campgrounds: those that offer electrical hook-ups, sewers and water at each site; those that offer one or two out of the list; and those that are primitive and offer none of the above. On top of these basics there might be swimming pools, river tubing, club houses, general stores, laundromats and theme parks. For the most part, I consistently chose state and national parks for their beauty, their relatively larger sites, and their affordability. These not-for-profit parks were in designated conservation areas, held in trust for the public, and well maintained by the park services. Their scenery and natural offerings of beaches, water recreation, and hiking made those parks especially ideal for someone like me who was seeking space and peace in which to reflect and create.

Private campgrounds, on the other hand, are the livelihood of the owners. So it makes sense that they crowd as many campsites as possible onto their land. They advertise more, entice families with Disney-like promises, and frequently charge more.

On the other end of the continuum, however, are the private RV resorts which offer all of the hook-ups, including on-line for your computer, as well as a host of other comforts you might find at any resort: clubhouse, restaurants, golf course, or indoor pool for inclement weather. The night before I met my kids at the Hilton Head condo, I stayed at an RV resort where each site fronted the water and had its own dock and pier with an onsite four-star French restaurant. What I wouldn't have given to be back there that cold night in Louisiana instead of waiting in line to sign in at a KOA.

"It's not supposed to be this cold in Louisiana," I shouted while I pounded on the steering wheel. "I'm supposed to be eating etouffe or peeling boiled shrimp! Camping in a luscious grove listening to patois!" Unfortunately, the people next to me did not know I was having a mild tantrum and thought I was in trouble.

They signaled for me to lower my window. "Having car trouble, sugar?" came the sweet question.

Embarrassed, I shook my head. "Just been a long, cold day, that's all."

Satisfied that I was okay, the couple settled in for a chat. We exchanged the usual weather commentary, how far we'd driven, where we were from, how many kids and grandkids we had, and how was I doing this alone, all the while inching forward to claim a spot for the night.

"It's the holidays, you know," the couple continued. "Every place is crowded, and we're all a bit overdone what with the hoopla and the partying. Too much, if you know what we mean?" I smiled and nodded. "We're getting as far away for the next few weeks as we can. Love the grandkids, but it's time for us to have some sun and fun!" He jiggled his eyebrows in a mock leer and got from me something I thought I had forgotten how to do. Laugh.

I asked them where they were going to find such things. "Oh this bad spell of weather can't last. We're headed for Florida. Go there every year. Some great campgrounds on the island beaches." Again the eyebrows drew a laugh from me and a slap on the wrist from his wife. I wished them well as I finally arrived at the first spot in line and looked ahead at the over-crowded sea of RV's, pop-ups, converted vans and tents. It was the most unaesthetic, flat, treeless campground I had ever seen. Just the thing to finish off the day!

I tried to be philosophical about it as I backed onto a six foot wide slab jammed so tightly against my neighbors that if I opened my awning I would be touching their backside. Unfortunately that worked both ways. I wouldn't be eating outside in the cold anyway.

I plugged in the tiny Wal-Mart ceramic heater I had no faith would heat up anything more than my toes, and immediately turned on the lights to dispel the damp gray darkness. My only goal was to quickly make my bed with a thick comforter, and snuggle down to snack. It was time to try to meditate myself out of the icy fog I had allowed to take over the inside of both the Falcon and myself. My journal was no help. I managed to write only the barest facts about the cold day and the long drive from Florida to Baton Rouge to the KOA. When I thought of being with Sam last night in Panama City, I almost wept. Then I turned on the news and really wept.

War in the Middle East was hourly coming closer to reality. At home snowstorms were blanketing the country from northern California to the east coast. Highways closed in Flagstaff; even Tucson was cold. High winds and drifts were recorded all across the country. I hated being so self-absorbed, but honestly, could I have picked a worse year to be stuck in a camper? It was time for some serious centering and reminding myself what I was about, or I was in danger of losing my focus. I had come too far, learned too much to allow myself to be swayed off my path by the mere threats of winter, maybe passing up the love of my life, and having no place to go.

I remembered a meditation that I had written down last summer inspired by a Lau Tzu[9] book Richie insisted I have for my trip. I scrambled around to find what I had written, registering with pleasant surprise that the van was now toasty warm. I grabbed a hidden bag of chocolate cookies and settled down to take stock of my flagging energy and courage. What was really going on here?

At the outset, I knew that when I made a commitment to trust the voice of God to lead me in this life, I was going to have to go into interior places of the soul that I would just as soon not venture. For the last several days I had been avoiding delving into my own murky depths for all the usual reasons. The process required a look at my own demons, to expose the deliberately hidden parts. Dragging them into consciousness is nauseatingly sweaty work. The results of enlightened self-knowledge are worth it, but the process never beckons lightly.

I have a fantasy that this process is practice for when we cross over from life into the hereafter. God will gravely ask, "Are you willing to have a spotlight thrown on your entire life, to see and know it all, in every detail, every thought, action, interaction and motivation?" As in life, the choice will be ours to yay or nay.

When I was a child I wondered why Jesus said that many would turn away from the light. Now that I have lived longer, I understand. Becoming intimate with God means becoming intimate with myself. It means standing in the divine spotlight where there is no place or desire to hide. It means knowing and being known. It is the only way to flush the illusions; it is the only way to stand in the presence of God, the Unconditional Lover who sees it all and loves us anyway.

What I had been avoiding was looking at the hurt places in my psyche that had emotionally stunted me, that prevented me from engaging in healthy relationships. The holidays exposed my vulnerabilities, my dependence on the illusion of relationships as *external* prescriptions for inner peace and happiness. How ironic that I had hit the road to explore living from the inside out, yet part of me continued to operate out of the belief that an external person could make my life if not perfect, then certainly better. If I could convince an emotionally unavailable person to love me, then I could *fix* the hole in my soul, make up for all the emotional unavailability I had lived with in my lifetime, and ultimately know that I am whole. In essence, I had a habit of turning my wholeness over to the very people least able to provide what I needed. Their needs always took precedence.

No surprise that I was cranky with depleted energy. It wasn't the weather. It was the storm inside myself. Breathing deeply from the center of a lonely frigid squall, I sought the comfort of my spiritual compass in a meditation written in August but somehow synchronistically was meant for the winter to come.

WHEN ENERGY IS LOW:
- **return to breathing**
  (focus on the elements of breathing; visualize the breath as light and air rushing to fill every part of my body; deepen the center with each breath)
- **return to patterns of creation**
  (focus on the patterns of the natural world; visualize the images of shells, leaves, the bark on trees, snowflakes, rivers, the swirls on the wings of butterflies; see the incredible wholeness of creation in the patterns of detail)

- **return to life's stream**
  (focus on the natural flow of time, energy, age; I am right where I am supposed to be at this moment)
- **return to the Creative Power that is in all things**
  (focus on the energy, light and love that is the Source of all, that is the same spark of life in all Creation)
  THEN:
- **listen to the Voice Within that calls my name**
  (wait with an attitude of anticipation; sink into the silence; expect to hear)
- **listen to the harmony of the universe that echoes in my inner place**
  (wait quietly for that peaceful moment when my inner and outer strivings are at one)
- **listen to the leading of God who tells me which path is mine**
  (wait in quietness and confidence that I will know which direction God is sending)
  FINALLY:
- **learn the way of gratitude**
  (practice being grateful for everything; saying "thank you" is a simple act of pure worship available at every moment)
- **sing the praises of each day**
  (practice being aware of each moment and rejoicing in thought and song)
- **pray for guidance in all ways**
  (practice the habit of aligning my thoughts and actions with the Divine)
  THEN YOU WILL:
- **Love Being**

When energy and spirits are low there are six words to live by: *return, listen, learn, sing, pray* and *love. How hard could that be?* I asked myself as I reached over to turn out the lights. As I lay there in the dark, the crumbs from the guilty pleasure cookies irritated my new found peace. Throwing off the covers, I swept out the bed, picked the empty bag up off the floor and prayed that I would not have to leave the Falcon to find a restroom in the middle of a dark and stormy night. I grabbed a bucket from underneath the storage benches in the back just in case nature called, for nothing in this world could convince me to go out in the freezing rain to find the bathhouse. Then I remembered that I had not set up the coffee for the morning. I had been so anxious to open up the bed and burrow in that I hadn't taken the time to organize all the items that an open bed blocked from retrieving. My equilibrium was once more at risk.

Bowing to the inevitable, I got up, pushed my bed half-way back into sofa-mode and proceeded to do things decently and in order. I flipped on the five-inch TV to listen to the late news while I cleaned, made coffee, and remade the bed. Once again I sent up a prayer for Sam and his guys, knowing that they were mobilizing for deployment to the Gulf.

The weather was still a mess everywhere except—where? I scrambled to pay attention. Southern Texas. When a map of the state was flashed up on the screen, I had that familiar lifting of my inner spirits that signaled something I needed to pay attention to. Where in the world was Brownsville, Texas? I had to walk over the darn bed again to find my maps and atlas somewhere up front between the seats. I had never heard of it, but I knew without a doubt that that was where I was headed.

According to my maps, I was going a long way down, almost to the Mexican border. I laughed out loud. Brownsville was very close to a place called South Padre Island, right in the Gulf of Mexico. Maybe I wasn't finished with beaches yet, after all.

As I drifted off to sleep I made a mental note to call my parents. I knew that my dad's sister and her family lived in Texas. Although I had not seen them for years, dad stayed in touch and kept me informed. It was just one of those things about our geographically distanced family. My generation depended on *others* to keep us up to date. Maybe I could detour off to catch-up lives with them.

I snuggled down into my warm comforter renewed, recommitted, and reenergized. What I couldn't know then, of course, was that it wasn't only beaches I was not finished with. I decided that I could really Love Being.

Chapter 13
Closer Walk

Heirlooms we don't have in our family. But stories we've got.
Rose Cherin

The only warmth I could find that first week in January was at my aunt and uncle's home in Dallas. They had been living in Texas most of my married life. Though I had fond memories of the few times we had been in each other's company, I was suddenly nervous. I really did not know my family, yet here I was asking to be taken in.

"Why young lady, you get yourself right on over here," was enticement enough to draw me deeper into Texas. Anyone who called me a young lady was on my list of favorites. By the time I arrived, icy rains were slicking city streets, causing local drivers to throw hissy fits. Where were the salt and sand trucks that by now should have been blanketing the roads? If I had wanted winter driving, I would have stayed in New England.

However, from the moment I entered my Aunt Waneta, ("that's Waneta with a W," she says without drawing a breath), and Uncle Chuck's house, I was enveloped in the cozy warmth of hugs, food, storytelling and music. I felt like I was sitting in a steaming hot tub in the middle of a blizzard.

"You know that story, don't you Jeanie? About mom leaving the farm in West Virginia and making her way to Martins Ferry and going into service cooking for a doctor's family, which is something you should appreciate being married to a doctor and all. Except, oh my, divorce is something, isn't it? Our Ross is divorced, you know, but mom, bless her heart, isn't here to see it. But she came down out of the hills and cooked for that family, and that's where she met dad who was still living with his family down along the Ohio River. Well, Rose and Ross courted for a while, then Rose brought her little sister down and she met dad's brother and before long the third sister came and she met Ross's other brother and before you know it all three sisters married all three brothers…"

"There were three of them?" I ask, breathing for her. "I knew about Uncle Frank and Aunt Nora, but I didn't know about the others."

"Well, you moved away so soon after your daddy left school, so you probably haven't heard all the stories and remember we called him Uncle Shrank because he was so short…"

"And he had a funny-looking finger on one hand…"I tagged in.

"…from an accident up to the mill…but he was a good soul and one of dad's brothers and he had three kids and they would come up to the Old Brick, that's what we called our house, you know…

"But I really want you to tell me about Uncle Leroy," I broke in. "All I ever heard was that he stole a streetcar once and went to prison."

"'Oh, oh,' Mom would always say. 'Lookee here now, lookee here, poor Leroy couldn't help the way he was. He was unjustly accused.' And, Jeanie, we would all laugh while Mama Rose chased us around the kitchen trying to hush us up because we all knew her brother was the biggest con man in six counties, traveling through the hills, when he needed cash, holding tent meetings, preaching and saving souls for the collection plate. He stole the street car to *escape* the police who were chasing him for stealing a monkey wrench!" And here we broke into peals of laughter, right on cue the way we had always done at the dumb absurdity of our gene pool.

What a family, I think, not for the first time. I heard myself laughing at the only slightly exaggerated stories of those exotic creatures as if they were characters out of a book, not my own genetic heritage. These were my grandparents and my great aunts and uncles; their blood flowed through my veins and kept my heart beating. They were not 'out there' somewhere in the universe wherever the past dwells. They were 'in here' dwelling right alongside all the other bits and pieces of the simmering stockpot that makes up my life. I laughed to myself as the irony hit me. Who among us can take a trip into our own future without confronting our own past? Is that what I was doing there in Dallas?

The next day, my cousins stopped by with their kids, and the stories began again when Aunt Waneta with a W held center stage. The rooms of her house filled up with her racing grandchildren tearing around the legs of adults who shared the family quirk of all talking at once. Every so often someone would yell out, "Tell about the picnic and the bananas…" And we would all quiet down, spellbound while Aunt Waneta's lilting semi-southern voice painted vivid emotional pictures of our moms' and dads' childhoods spent surviving the ravages of Depression poverty.

"Well, you see, we didn't have any money in those days, cause dad had lost his job up at the steel mill. 'Up to the mill' he called it. Jeanie, your dad and Aunt Ruth, the twins, were in high school and so was Uncle Dode. The other twins, Herald and Harrison, were in junior high; I was in sixth grade and Aunt Kathleen was a baby and Jerry wasn't born yet. Knowing we didn't have money for treats, somebody had given mom a bunch of bananas, so she decided that we should celebrate our good fortune by loading up the wagon and going up the hill to have a picnic by the creek. Now, there was no food in the house except for some old onions and some bread, but this wasn't a problem for Mama Rose. She got us all whipped up about the fun we would have, the games we would play and the wonderful bananas we would eat. There was a whole banana for each one of us! We were giggling and laughing while we made up a batch of onion sandwiches and tucked them in a basket with the precious fruit. Daddy Ross threw an old blanket over the basket, we all piled into the wagon and sang and laughed our way to the top of the hill." Here, a dramatic pause while we all held our breath knowing what was coming.

"We jumped down out of that wagon. Mom directed Russell, the oldest son, to carry the treasured basket. Jeanie, we all knew your daddy was going to be a preacher from the time he was six years old. He was the good guy, the one we could count on and trust to carry the bananas. He pulled back the blanket and there was Dode, caught with the basket on his lap, polishing off the last banana!"

Like always, there was a gasp in the room over such perfidious audacity. One of the horrified little ones predictably asked, "Did he really eat 'em all, Memaw?" as the implications of such monumental betrayal sank in.

One of the older ones chimed in with, "I woulda' killed him!" But Aunt Waneta's eyes crinkled with remembered joy as she laughed while she told us how the whole gang tackled Dode in a great free-for-all and Rose waded in, arms swinging, shouting "Lookee here! Lookee here!" as she pulled her offspring apart and the whole group fell down laughing.

"After all," Aunt Waneta said, "we still had our onion sandwiches, games to play, and songs to sing." And of course, a story to tell almost sixty years later that never failed to confront its hearers with that elusive, yearned for alternate universe where siblings forgave, parents were reconciled to devastating financial need, and laughter and singing were a loving family's antidotes to sorrow. Could it be?

My cousins and I made eye contact, then quickly glanced away as if we could not bear to see our self doubts mirrored on the other's face. I imagined that we each questioned in our hearts whether or not, given the same circumstances, we would have been as creatively faithful to all being well.

In addition to eternal optimism, my dad and all his siblings shared one glorious talent. They could play by ear any musical instrument they picked up. And everybody sang. There was not one family gathering of this clan that did not end with everyone gathered around the piano and singing four part harmony "until the little ones slept and the big ones wept."

Following tradition, the Dallas evening ended with Aunt W at the piano playing while the rest of us sang along. *Three Blind Mice* and *Jesus Loves Me* for the little guys segued into *Danny Boy* and other ballads, and from there inevitably segued into spirituals and old hymns. One after the other we sang those marvelous tunes which over the years had touched our hearts and taught each soul how to sing in harmony. No matter where our theology or practices had taken us, we all rallied when the old hymns rolled out.

I looked around the room glorying in the piping sounds emanating from the little ones, the rich variety of tones from the two professional musicians among us, as well as the young law student and his younger sister, and from the grand matriarch and patriarch of this Texas part of my clan. We had bass, tenor, alto and soprano in a harmonic mix fit for the heavenly choir. For those brief moments the music blended this far-flung disparate group into a close and loving family. I chuckled as I imagined Rose and Ross hovering nearby marveling at how far we had all come from cooking for the doctor.

The hymn singing transported me to vague memories of being in my grandparents' living room where too many extroverts always crowded into too little space. Where the mixed cacophony of screaming kids, mothers shouting, and dads booming out orders bulged the roof. The Old Brick's rusty façade, built precariously into a hillside in Martins Ferry, Ohio, was filled to bursting with the stories of a way of life we had all left far, far behind in the old river valley. That night in Dallas, the musical evening ended with the usual family ritual signaled by someone suggesting that it was time to sing Rose's favorite. In a way, this is what we had all been anticipating. The other songs were the warm-up.

Just a closer walk with Thee;
Grant it, Jesus, is my plea,
Daily walking close to Thee,
Let it be, dear Lord, let it be.

Not a bad song for someone who wants to live from the inside out. For the first time, I wondered if this was my grandmother's way of exploring her inner life. We never had a conversation about why she was so drawn to this song, what pulled on her, where it took her in the depths of her being. She was just my loving old grandma, rosy cheeked, talking up a storm till she stuttered, full of "lookee here's" while she ran around her kitchen, making us all laugh. Treating her with the unconscious condescension of childhood, I didn't take the time or have

132

the perspicacity to know who she really was. Now I only had stories to keep her real. She never traveled farther from the Old Brick than to my parents' home in Indiana in her lifetime. Yet I sensed in Dallas that she and I shared the same quest to 'walk closer.' I could hear her rich alto harmonizing with my melody in this simple song of spiritual faith that affirms being on the road, getting older, heading out and never being alone.

Wow. I almost missed being there in Dallas. If the weather hadn't interfered, I might have kept right on going west and missed this circling back to my roots and origins that helped me make sense of my past. I found new meanings in extended family relationships and tested the waters of inherited companions on my journey.

If I hadn't known it before, I was learning it then. Life is not linear. It circles and circles until we learn our lessons, or learn what we need to keep going in the great dance. I looked in the mirror and saw the blue eyes and pink cheeks of Grandma Rose. Even my hair has turned a lighter shade of *champagne*, like hers.

When I talk to strangers about their deepest longings, or tell a story of my life to an audience, or sing a song spontaneously in the super market, or embarrass my children by singing along in an elevator; when I giggle inappropriately in quiet places, or chat on and on seemingly without drawing breath, I see Aunt Waneta, Aunt Ruth, Uncle Harold, Uncle Dode, Jerry, my Dad, and a whole host of ghostly relatives too numerous to name. Many of them are gone now, but the stories remain.

Who will tell the stories about me? And what stories will they choose to tell? How well will the stories they relate reflect the real *me*? Soon, inevitably, I will be the grandmother.

Chapter 14
New Game

The Falcon and I were eager to head out despite the cold. For hours after we left Dallas I could point my nose toward my shoulder for a wiff of the fried breakfast Aunt Waneta and Uncle Chuck insisted I eat at dawn. I loved listening to the byplay between those loyal lovers of fifty plus years. I was content watching her scootch around the kitchen waving a spatula while she popped, flipped, scooped and served. I loved catching them in their private moments of shared contact when the softening of eyes and kissy mouths belied the stinging words exchanged over food consumption.

I was more than full of fried eggs and bacon that cold morning. So I made facile promises to stay in touch, to be careful on the road, all the while wondering if I would be a better niece in the future. I also made a silent promise to myself that I was ready for some lighthearted fun. My psyche was so sated by the cumulative joys and learnings of the holiday season that I felt like a semi-comatose glutton who could barely move after the holiday feast. You would think I could learn a lesson or two about not tempting fate.

As I drove farther and farther south in continued icy rain, I forced myself to breathe deeply, to trust that I was headed in the right direction. I repeated the words out loud three times, *"I trust that I am going in the right direction. I trust that I am going in the right direction. I trust that I am going in the right direction."*

Someone had written in a book somewhere that anything repeated out loud three times forges a convolution in the brain and we have it as a permanent part of our reality. So I repeated it several more times in batches of three just to make sure, for the driving that day rivaled the Chesapeake Bay Bridge for keeping my heart in my throat.

The wind, rain and sleet blasted the side of the Falcon. All my mental and muscle focus was concentrated on keeping the top-heavy van lumbering straight down the highway. Sightseeing was limited to the white line down the center of the road. I barely noticed when I passed from urban landscape to the vast horizons for which the state is famous. I simply wanted to get *there*, wherever I was supposed to be. Reminding myself one more time that I was following my inner voice, and that I was exactly where I was *supposed* to be, I continued on down Route 77 through Harlingen headed for Brownsville.

The weather must have eased up a bit, for I found myself practicing my high school and college Spanish by reading the musically exotic names printed on the road signs. Mesmerized by the endless gray ribbon stretching out ahead, I fell into my favorite mind game of making up stories about those places and the people who lived there. It helped to pass the monotony of long distance driving and helped edge out the anxiety that hovered just below the surface of my awareness.

Agua Dulce *means sweet water. Out there in the middle of nowhere was a small natural spring that saved the lives of a shattered family, chased inland from the waters of the gulf by a tyrannical land-grabber. After years of merely surviving (thanks to the agua dulce) it became a way station for the early Mexican traders working their way north. Later it saved the lives of settlers heading west in their Conestoga wagons, fainting from disease and thirst in the smothering heat of a Texas sun. Agua dulce was a lifesaving miracle of the westward expansion.* I named the family, married off *las hijas* to men who were *muy guapo*; made sure *los hijos* grew into stalwart protectors of their fathers' legacies and this awesome land through which I was now time-traveling.

Farther south, *Rancho Viejo* grabbed my mind. *Did that mean an old ranch that had been there since the beginning of maps? Or did it mean that it was a ranch where only white haired people worked? I could see it all. A vivid picture of hordes of old folk with sombreros and bright scarves riding horses in the scorching sun, hoeing gardens, baking bread in the outside ovens. I saw them dancing at fiestas, drinking tequila in cantinas, and keeping time with the mariachis. Hey, maybe this was the original assisted living arrangement. Sign up now for Rancho Viejo where you can stay active at work and play as long as you can stand or stand it!*

One glance in the rearview mirror reminded me that the color of my hair would soon qualify me for a starring role in my own fairy tale, which was not an amusing thought.

My elaborate fantasizing accomplished its purpose, for just ahead was the sign for Brownsville, one of the southernmost towns in the United States of America, and the warmest place in the whole country, thank God. Finally I drew breath as I realized that I had outrun the horrors of wind and sleet.

Just as it had a week earlier on the other side of the Gulf, the weakened sun broke through strongly enough to cast the first shadows I had seen since Florida. A little giddy euphoria threatened when I consciously unwound my fingers from the steering wheel to let the blood flow back into my aching hands. For the first time in hours I had the luxury of looking around. I must say that Brownsville was a disappointment.

What had I expected? There were no pine trees on the map of Brownsville. It is a city with malls, shops, busy traffic patterns, street lights and the bustle of commerce. If I kept going south I was going to be in Mexico in a very short moment. Brownsville was right smack on the Rio Grande River where you could look across into the faces of another country. That sobered me up in a hurry. Now that I was here, where was I to go?

The mall I pulled into looked familiar at first glance. It was like any strip mall anywhere. At second glance, I saw that most of the stores had Spanish signage. *Mercado, Pandaria, Carneceria*[10] and something with *Ropa* in it which I had forgotten meant clothing, not rope. I rolled down the window and the music pounding out of cars and buildings were Latino songs. The breezy smells of cumin and cilantro mixed with charcoaled meats (*carne a la parrilla*) tempted me with juicy longings for authentic Mexican food. The people were friendly, waving to one another, chatting openly, dressed in a rainbow of colors, a complete contrast from the understated sidewalk life in New England. Teenagers, with their droopy shorts and oversized tees, were the only anchor of normality in an unfamiliar landscape. The realization of how far I was from all that was familiar hit my stomach with the hard knowledge that I was truly away, out of my element, out of my culture.

Then I stopped. "Wait a minute," I said out loud. "This is my culture, too. I am a part of this." We are a country of diverse cultures. We all share the same humanity. Yes, I am out of my known element, but I am not out of my country, nor my species, nor my spiritual home. I was led here. This is the great adventure I've been seeking! Slowly I grinned while I tried to take in all the sights, sounds and smells at once.

The elemental gift of traveling is to stretch yourself out, away, to create a tension of new ideas, shapes and forms. To rub yourself against the band that holds you in place until you slough your old dead cells in favor of growing into a new skin. That day, I knew I had pulled the rubber band about as taut as it could go. So with that mental kick in the rear, I ordered two tacos to go, (one beef and one chicken with, *por favor, frijoles refritos* in the shell with just a few *jalapenos, gracias*) and wolfed them down while I took out my maps. There, just slightly north and east of Brownsville exactly where the Holy Spirit guided me was a green pine tree, right on the coast. Amen.

II
Outdoor Resorts

Port Isabel is a small town on the land side connected to South Padre Island by a causeway. I could tell immediately that I would be able to get around very easily with my bicycle. Canals threaded the landscape making it possible for small boats to navigate inland from the Gulf. Not far from the bridge was a huge Outdoor Resorts, similar to the one on Hilton Head, except here every RV site was either on the golf course or on a canal with its own dock.

The woman at the check-in center handed me a calendar of events starting with a *singles* dinner the very next night. I did not even bother to check in with my inner voice. I assumed this was the right place.

When she saw that I was from Massachusetts, the woman behind the counter wondered, "Do you know folks from Connecticut? They're right across from you."

I almost blurted out that I live *two hours* away from Connecticut and there are probably people in my town who have never been so far. Then I remembered where I was. Two hours in Texas was probably a short drive for dinner. So I smiled and told her that I would be anxious to meet these Connecticut neighbors. She had one more comment before she let me go.

"There was another single woman in here a while back. Nice and friendly. Some folks thought she was a bit too friendly. Do you know her? She's pretty young, though; on her way to California."

"Was she pulling a Mercedes?" I asked head down, signing the credit card receipt.

"She sure was!"

"Going to take a new job in California?" I looked up and grinned.

"Say! Is she a friend of yours?" she looked me over more critically. I figured I'd better put some distance between me and the elusive single female who was marking the trail ahead of me.

"Actually, no, I've never met her, wouldn't know her if I fell over her. But she sure has made an impression on everybody in the camping world."

"Well, we're not supposed to talk out of school about our renters, but seein' how you know all about her anyway…" she paused waiting for a sign from me to shake or nod, "I will say that she was the California type, if you get my meanin'?"

I really did, but I hated to admit it even to myself. But the conversation was too rich to end it with a righteous discourse on stereotyping and gossip. And being the canny therapist that I was, I could make a pretty good stab at what the Texas Belle was hinting at anyway. I might as well let her finish. She was clearly dying to impart some juicy bits. So I merely smiled again and she took that as permission.

"Well," she leaned over the counter, "that girl had herself a time here at the Resorts and in town with the singles group. Bein' young, havin' a Mercedes and not too bad lookin' she like to tore up some romances around here. She was forever inviting men over to her RV. Lord only knows what they were doin' in there. Not that it's any of our business, but one of the engaged couples got disengaged and lit outta here before their month was up. Wooee, she could dance up a storm and hold her liquor, they said."

"Thanks for the map of the resort," I told her while packing up all the paperwork and brochures. "You've been very helpful," I smiled mendaciously. Truthfully, she would take up a lot of space in my journal that night. She got one more lick in before I hit the door laughing.

"Be sure to go to the singles dinner tomorrow night. You'll be meetin' some wonderful people, most of them just about your age." I assumed she meant not young.

"Right," I muttered as I toss a wave over my shoulder and depart the premises. It couldn't have been clearer. Single women traveling alone are a little suspect anyway, so be on your guard and don't do anything to give them stories to tell when you leave.

On the other hand, why not? Okay, I confess. I was wondering what my predecessor did in her RV with those guys. Oh well, the Falcon was a great chaperone. It was too small to do much of anything, or at least to do *that,* whatever it was *she* was doing in her RV. Give it up.

Trying to keep one eye on the map, I drove down suburban looking streets, past permanent doublewides beautifully landscaped with colorful annuals tumbling out of planters. I wound around an extensive light brick complex in the middle of the resort that had to be the club house. The woman at the front desk proudly told me there were rooms for geology lectures, sewing machines, crafts, library and other activities, as well as a large recreation room for line dancing lessons, plays, and the weekly bridge groups and dinner dances. At the end of the clubhouse closest to where I would be, she had said, pre gossip session, "Look for the windows of the coffee shop and restaurant." Was I in paradise?

Constrained by my usual need to be near a bath house, I rented a spacious site on the golf course across the street from a canal. Neighbors were not on top of each other there. In fact, the Falcon seemed a little lonely on the giant slab designed for the much longer, pricier RV's. The force of the wind forbore putting up the awning which might have added a little bit of cachet to my plain turtle shell. I noticed that none of the large RV's, trailers and fifth-wheels had their much sturdier awnings up, nor did anyone have the usual outdoor furniture displayed. That was a little ominous.

Despite the elements, however, I seemingly had landed in a place that did not appear to depend on such trivialities for enjoyment. Meditative walks on the beach receded to a closet in my inner sanctum with the door slowly closing. It was time to put this new self out in the world, to experience a community where I am simply me without the accoutrements of my former identity and roles. There was no one to please here but myself.

I paid in advance for a whole month and felt that it was not a risk at all. I would be living a very different lifestyle this winter from the State Parks and beaches of the fall.

Chapter 15
A Foot in Two Worlds

I'm having a tough time staying on my path these days. There are so many levels of issues demanding attention. There is the war, the constant social life, and my need to pull back into prayer and meditation. My efforts to write, my subject matter, seems so puny when juxtaposed to what is happening in the world. The incredible stupidity of war, any war, as a way to solve problems staggers me.

Journal: Texas, January

I wonder if there are twenty [people] alive in the world now who see things as they really are. That would mean that there were twenty [people] who were free, who were not dominated or even influenced by any attachment to any created thing or to their own selves...I don't believe that there are twenty such [people] alive in the world. But there must be one or two. They are the ones who are holding everything together and keeping the universe from falling apart.

Thomas Merton: *Seeds of Contemplation*[11]

Like the weather, that winter in coastal Texas was a jumble of inconsistencies: humidity, fog, and rain with just enough sun breaking through to pump up false expectations and relief. The Gulf war was the main topic of conversation in every social gathering, with the pros and cons pretty much secretly divided along gender lines.

I ostensibly lounged in the coffee shop after my morning walks to read the paper, but in truth I was there to listen to the irreverent band of older Peter Pans spin their tales. With their sparse white hair and seamy leathery faces these were men in their 70's and 80's who had served in either WWII or Korea. They sat around each morning critiquing the military reports of the day before, strategically planning the next military maneuvers, and apparently every bit as pumped as Sam's recruits. Unrepentantly eavesdropping, I thought that they were not nearly as belligerent about Saddam as they were about sending females into action. Or maybe it was all a show for the benefit of the one single woman who dared to breach their space.

"We gotta support our troops, but darn, they should keep women behind the lines. Not be putting them in harm's way," White Whiskers swiped his hand across the table.

"Can you imagine what would have happened at Normandy or Midway if we had to rely on females to get through that surf to land?" agreed his pal. "The water woulda' taken care of them long before the enemy."

"Swept off their feet!" A chorus of *hoo-boys* and suggestive grins took over.

"Women do the nursing, men do the fighting. What's wrong with that?" begged a voice of reason. "What do they want, for crying out loud?" This from a man who probably never read Freud.

"How could you trust them to back you up? What if she broke a nail?" Big belly laughs were probably more for the effect on those of us hog tied to our chairs than for real.

More soberly White Whiskers concluded, "I've got to say, war is one big roller coaster ride from dizzying excitement to being boring as hell." There were grim nods all around. This time no one made eye contact as coffee cups were put to use.

The women I swam with, some of them spouses of the old soldiers, while publicly supporting their men, would often bemoan the shortsighted thinking that war ever solves anything. These women, no longer the cheering sweethearts and first wives of young soldiers, were now the mothers and grandmothers of fighting troops. We lolled against the side of the pool each day letting our legs float to the surface while we kibitzed.

Someone eventually asked, "Did you see the news last night? I could barely stand it watchin' all those young people leavin' for war."

"Did you see that momma in her fatigues hangin' onto her baby and both of them cryin'?" Moans of agreement swept over the water.

"What got me was watching both the mother and the father saying goodbye to their poor scared little kids while the grandparents just stood there looking like their hearts were breaking," I inserted. That hushed our chatting for a few seconds until another voice dropped into the quiet.

"Hank and I are going home today." A chorus of protests echoed in the pool room. "We just got a call this morning. Our son is off to Kuwait. What else can we do? His wife can't give up her job while he's gone, so we'll be helping out with Julie, Mickey and the baby." We all stopped talking and looked at Marie from Kansas who was forcing us to confront the reality that this war hit close to home. "First he was in Viet Nam and I didn't close my eyes at night for almost two years. Now this." Tears joined the chlorinated droplets on her cheeks.

"Our grandson leaves next week," commiserated Barbara from Michigan. "But our daughter says not to cut our winter short. Shoot, in our RV, we'd hardly make it home in time to say goodbye anyway. So we're talking to him on the phone as often as possible. I can't believe he's old enough to go." She swept her hand through the water as though she could swim out of her sadness and confusion. "My husband tries to act like this is a great opportunity for David to serve his country, but I can tell he's scared underneath." She looks off in the distance. "You know, it's like it's bringing stuff up he wants to stay hidden."

"Yeah," agreed the quietest one, "my guy is getting quieter and quieter, too. I think the only time he wants to talk war anymore is when he's with the café group. I know he's kept a lot to himself about Korea…"

"Mine, too. He was in Italy during the big bloody push north and I tell you, he zips up about the rah-rah of war when the talk turns to that part of the world," echoed another.

The oldest one among us lets us know that her first husband was killed during that bloody push in Italy. "I know how important it is to serve your country," she said with all the gravity of her age and experience, "but you would think that one war would be enough for one family in one generation. Isn't that written in the Bible somewhere?"

Even if it were, I thought with sadness, *would anyone heed?*

No one used the peace word. No one could quite bring themselves to say that peace is a good thing, a desirable state, a cause worth putting all our efforts behind. Yet each one was scared of the alternative, frightened for the personal cost to themselves and the collective, and frustrated at the necessity for tearing apart families while facing the despair of pain and death. No one in that southern Texas town wanted to be perceived as anything other than patriotically supportive while we risked the lives of our young. Off and on for the rest of the day I prayed for the safety of the families of the women at the pool, for Sam and his boys, for all the troops I watched on TV, and for the folly of war.

That night I dreamed a strange and haunting dream. I was adrift in the crisply blackened night sky, hovering at the top of the universe, shuffling among the faceted glowing stars, only dimly aware of the world below. In slow motion I exuberantly reached toward the stars as they drifted over my fingers, bounced off my toes, and gently tickled my face in a fantasy of gentle delight. A fragrant rose appeared, deeply densely pink and not yet quite opened. "What is a rose doing here?" I asked in some surprise. Though oddly out of place, I could not help but notice how wrenchingly beautiful it was in contrast to the black and white of the night heavens. Its beauty stung my eyes. In the way of dreams, my question was answered. "The rose is your prayer for your enemy. Pray for Saddam."

I awoke with the suddenness of the soul jumping back into the body, eyes fully opened and trained on the ceiling, hyper-aware of the van, yet oddly disoriented in time and place. The tears on my face bore silent testimony to the reality of the dream, and for a few seconds my nose followed the vanishing scent of perfumed air. I did not question the rationale nor dissect the dream. I simply closed my eyes and held onto the rose, free for the first time to drift in the cosmos of universal prayers for all humanity. Perhaps for a few hours I was one of those holding the universe together.

The singles group quickly became my point of reference. From formal activities to informal gatherings there was something happening every day. One of the events any of us missed at our social peril was the weekly meeting for Tex-Mex and dancing at one of the smoky local bars. It was a chance to safely accept the attentions of a variety of men; to play at flirting without strings. One of my rules was that I always stayed with the group. I had not been in this environment for thirty years. It was just plain too easy to become sixteen again. It was one thing to flirt harmlessly from the safety of marriage, but quite another, I was learning, to flirt unattached. There were times when I felt that all the sophistication of travel, education, motherhood and wifedom had been no preparation at all for my current life.

Men fell into two categories. There were those who were so dangerous they were safe. These were the guys whose values and lifestyles were so far removed from mine that as fascinating as their hedonistic, licentious actions were to rub against while dancing, I was never in any danger of taking them seriously.

"Hey, Yankee lady," the fortyish Texan drawled while walking toward our table. He was just under six feet tall and packed into worn jeans and cowboy boots. The sun had streaked his longish hair. He sported romantic stubble beneath his Paul Newman eyes. Every woman at our table looked up in anticipation that he was calling out to her. Unless, of course, she wasn't from up north. Which, of course, I was. I called on every bit of my dormant teenage flippancy when I tremblingly allowed him to lead me onto the floor. This man was truly dangerous.

"I been watchin' you, darlin'," he smiled down at me, "and you can dance...for a yankee." He grinned and winked causing me to laugh spontaneously at his outrageous ego. "But I think it's about time you learned the Texas two-step. Whadda ya think?"

Secretly, I have to say that I had been dying to learn the dance since seeing it in movies before Paul the Cowboy was born. There was something stately about the two-step, with the man's arm on top of the woman's shoulder, gently guiding her in a smooth waltz-like motion.

"Why, thank you, sir," I cooed back at *Paul*, "for taking the time to teach this poor Yankee lady all that you know." His eyes blinked. Then he roared laughing and spent the rest of the evening tutoring me to tunes like "Waltz Across Texas," and "All My Ex's Live in Texas." I had a momentary regret that, metaphorically, the minister and his wife still waited up for my teenage self when the evening waned. He sure was cute.

The other category of eligibles was men who were definitely looking for connection and possibly commitment. These were the ones I had to hold at arms length. They posed a danger of another sort. I was on a personal journey and could not afford to be taken off my path. I needed to learn how to live on my own inner strength before I was ready to become part of a couple again. I wanted to be able to bring a whole person into a relationship the next time. It soon became apparent, however, that that strength was being communicated out there and was attracting men whose mission it became to convince me that I really did not want to be alone. I wanted to take care of them.

Thomas took me to lunch in Matamoras, Mexico where we meandered lazily through the market place taking in the visual feast of colorful art, and glassware. I bought myself a pair of handmade sterling earrings sculpted in the shape of seashells that remind me to this day of all my months on beaches.

We sipped traditional margaritas made with fresh lime juice while we sat outside in the soft air waiting for our table. He talked about his grown children and his loneliness since his wife died. He asked me questions about my family and why I was divorced. It was comfortable to share similar values of family, education and the arts. My traveling alone was a bit of a mental stumbling block for him, but I had no emotional investment in convincing him to my point of view. All in all, it was a gentle, non-threatening, peaceful day. On the ride back to the resort something shifted.

He took his hand off the steering wheel and gave my knee a gentle squeeze. "This has been a momentous day for me," he smiled in my direction. I carefully smiled back wondering what in heaven's name he meant and where this was going. I lunged again for a little of the submerged teenager who knew how to head unwarranted declarations off before they were an embarrassment. He took his hand away.

"I sense that you and I have so much in common. We have so much together."

"Uh, yes. We both have grown children and we both know about loss," I quickly dithered. "There are lots of us, aren't there?" I throw out, trying to shunt the conversation onto a larger stage.

"Oh it's more than that," he states. "I know you're as lonely as I am. You're so brave. I think I'm **falling** in love with you. We will have a wonderful life together."

Panic filled my throat. He was going from one lunch date to a lifetime in Texas. I wanted to protest that I wasn't lonely. Well, maybe sometimes. But that was part of the deal, learning to live with the silence of aloneness and listening and waiting to integrate all of it into who I am. What I really needed to say was something else.

"I'm sorry, Thomas, but you don't really know me. I'm not lonely in the ways you describe. I'm not looking for someone to settle down with at this point. I still have the rest of the year to complete. A book to write."

Silence prevailed in the car until we reached the Falcon. I realized how true my words to Thomas were. I knew that I could not *settle* for having a man in my life ever again. No matter what the cost, I would not jump through hoops anymore just to be part of a couple. In my past life, I would have tried to make it better for Thomas, smooth over my rejection. I would have given him hope that someday he and I might have something if he still felt the same way in a year when my trip was over; when the rainbow turned upside down. But this time, I had to be honest with him and with myself. I might rue the day, but I had to be clear both within and without myself.

The days marched on with little change in weather or routine. Each day I recommitted myself to my *Intentions*, and continued to write purposefully for a book on women's spirituality. I walked or rode my bicycle when the weather was fair and swam in the indoor pool when it was not. The singles group continued dancing and eating, but the frenetic pace began to tug at my consciousness with the probes of boredom. Dressing to please, martinis before dinner, light-hearted banter, even political discussions began to pall. At times, when I was acquiescent long enough, I could hear echoes of that cold January night a year ago. *Everything is different but nothing has changed.* How easily I was falling back into a whirling social climate that had me out and about, but could not appease the restlessness of my seeking soul. I hollowly wondered if I were learning anything at all about living from the inside-out. My inner voice seemed to be lying somewhat fallow.

Fully intending to forgo some of the singles routine, I rededicated myself to the purpose of the trip and scheduled myself with a vengeance. Writing each day was a top priority. Naturally, that was when another man showed up.

We met at the singles' weekly event. Right there in the smoky bar we created an island of calm and refreshingly fell into an intellectual discussion of religion, politics and economic globalization. We both agreed that contrary to what our mothers told us, those were topics that should never be avoided. I learned that Justin's wife had died during the past summer and that he was recently retired from a college professorship. We walked the beach twice, expounding on our spiritual and religious beliefs and discovered that we were both PK's (preacher's kids). He asked me to dinner with some academic colleagues, a welcome contrast to singles night, in a grown-up restaurant with white tablecloths and folded napkins. Good food, interesting people, engaging conversation, and a quiet room; not a two-stepper in sight.

The next day a knock on the door interrupted the flow of my writing. I was on a roll and needed to concentrate for at least another two hours. But there was no place to hide in the van. It was Justin who fairly danced with suppressed excitement.

"I just had to tell you that I had a divine revelation, a spiritual understanding just like you were talking about," he blurted out the minute I opened the door. Not wanting to dampen his joy, I looked over my shoulder at the computer I longed to be in front of and mentally kissed my *roll* goodbye.

"What happened?" I asked.

"I woke up this morning," he said, "and a spiritual light came on and I knew that I love you." I promptly sat on the top step of the Falcon feeling a bit numb. Shock I think is what it is called. Before I could respond, not that there was a hint of response in me, he was off again. He leaned over and gave me a hug.

Cheerfully unaware of my catatonic state, he proceeded to state that the day was waiting. "I thought we could go shopping then take a walk on the beach and have lunch in town. Later we can talk about a trip I'd like for us to take to Alaska. I've always wanted to go there, but with Louise being sick for so long I could never make a plan. But now you and I can do it together. I thought we would take about three months for it sometime next year."

My brain was a whirligig. At least Justin had the sophistication to wait until after three dates to plan not only my day but the rest of my life! We hadn't even held hands. For a fraction of a second I calculated the advantages of having someone to travel with to Alaska, but then the cool hand of reason pressed down on my head and steadied my course. Before he could tell me that God told him to tell me that I should meekly fall in with the plan, I had to intervene on my own behalf.

First, I told him how honored I was. Then I explained that I wasn't available that day for lunch or beach walking, that I was working and needed to pay attention to my writing. I followed this with the gentle suggestion that perhaps he might want to consult with me before he made any plans, just to sort of check in and see if I had any thoughts, ideas, plans or persona of my own.

I did not delude myself that I had deeply hurt Justin's feelings. We had not known each other long enough or intimately enough for that. I may have wounded his pride if he felt my defense of self was a rejection of him. There would be some woman soon, I was certain, who would love to have her life planned, who would love to relinquish the role of decision-maker to Justin, and who, perhaps, would never care that he had difficulty knowing where his ego ended and hers began. Hallelujah, that woman was no longer me.

The weather started to improve slightly by the end of January, so I signed on for two more weeks while I prayed and waited and listened daily about where I was to go next. I assumed it would be Albuquerque or some place in New Mexico. Once again my assumptions were incorrect. The indications were *not yet,* whatever that meant. I went back to what worked best for me: listening in the silence for the inner voice, trusting and writing down what I heard, and being ready to act when it became clear.

Tucson. I was going to Tucson, Arizona for the remainder of the winter and the beginning of spring. I called my friend, Christine, who agreed to meet the Falcon and me there as our first houseguest from home. My juices were starting to flow again; I had something exciting to look forward to. Meanwhile, I tried to assess the final days of being in South Texas.

My brother, the biologist, rails against those writers and poets who insist on portraying winter as bleak, deadly, and frozen. A time when everything stops, motion is slowed, and there can be nothing better than to endure while anticipating the bursting, budding chaos of spring. "Not so," he loves to lecture. "Winter is the time of the greatest amount of fecund activity, planning, and putting in place of any season of the year. Under those leaves, under that snow, in the roots of all green things, in the caves and under mountains all life forms are fermenting, turning over, propagating in fantastic symbiosis to start the growing seasons of the earth. Winter," he says, "is the time of work; spring is the outcome of all the activity that came before." In my parlance, spring is the frosting on the cupcake; but winter *is* the cake.

While I packed up the Falcon for the next stage of our journey I contemplated what I was taking away from my time in Port Isabel, where it stacked up on the evolution of my reality scale. What were the lessons learned?

In my heart I knew that the most profound learnings need time to ferment and wend their way through the psyche to consciousness. Even so, I felt that I was missing something inside, something fecund and feisty, something alive that had me living in the growth of spiritual fulfillment since last January.

Somehow in Texas I felt that I was not as engaged in fully living from the inside out as I had experienced for the past year. I was feeling shallower, perhaps missing the focus of that whole year's grand plan. My words and thoughts were not as juicy and fecund as the days of water and beaches when I lived in the midst of poetic imagery.

So far, the winter in Texas had me whipping up the ingredients of my past: a pinch of family, a dash of values of war and peace, a fistful of men, and a generous amount of holes in my soul. In retrospect, that was an enormous batter of groundwork. If my brother were to be believed, my concerns about not being as spiritually alive as I was in the previous seasons were for naught. I was simply lying fallow, letting all the necessary work go on underground, letting my psyche and spirit get ready for all that frosting.

Book IV

Spring:
Arizona and New Mexico

Chapter 16
Transition—Again

Spring not only comes earlier to the desert than to the frosty forests and mountains of New England, it is far more subtle. When I left Port Isabel on February 15th, the air was crisp, the sky clear and the winds gentle enough to require only a sweatshirt to hold off the elements. I carefully laid the atlas on the passenger seat, plunked my water bottle in the cup holder, checked to make sure everything was bungeed down so that all flotsam and jetsam were secured where they could not take wing and distract me during the long drive ahead. My sap was up. I was ready to say goodbye and to hit the road to the next adventure.

According to my best estimation, I had at least two days driving simply to transverse the state of Texas and head south into New Mexico. Vague, unspecified anxiety streaking periodically through my comfort zone was the only disturbing sensation marring the day. Assuming that it was merely the ordinary excited nervousness that usually accompanied my stepping off into the unknown, I tried to push it below my emotional radar.

As mile after mile of flat barren land ticked by, I allowed the emptiness to creep into the hollow places of my spirit. This was the first time on the trip when my only goal was to cover as much ground as possible in a day. The sweep of the land began to toss my sentiments into a spiral of confusion where I questioned my inner voice yet again. I swallowed the heart stopping reality that *no one* in this universe knew where I was. I was utterly, totally, devastatingly alone in some of the most uncompromising land I had ever experienced. And there was no end in sight; the black highway stretched out forever.

Legs shaking with tension, I condemned Tucson to the other side of the world, for I could never cover enough of the endless vastness to get through it. Mile after mile after mile rolled on while I told myself that it was illogical not to go to Albuquerque, that New Mexico was closer. I desperately needed a closer goal. Surely that was a sensible strategy in the midst of overpowering vulnerability and fear?

Finally, I talked out loud to drum out the pitiful beatings of my thoughts and heart. I was not alone. Isolated, yes; but not alone. The words came out of my momentarily misplaced memories: "Look around you and what do you see? What is it that you can count on? Look at the world around you." Those same words had comforted me so many months ago with God's reminder that when I *see* there is always evidence of the steadfastness of the Creator.

I begged God for new eyes on that long arduous drive and slowly, very slowly began to unclench from the wheel to marvel at the land, breathtaking in its scenery and scope. Long, long vistas of open spaces graced by distant multiple ranges of purple mountains with names like Apache, Devil Ridge, Eagle and Quitman. Their peaks were at once gut-wrenchingly majestic, yet jagged and sharp like the teeth of fossilized giants. I had plenty of time to reflect on how easily ego and intellect overwhelmed my soul-knowledge when I allowed fear and mistrust to take over.

As I left the flat lands and gradually climbed higher, the mountains of west Texas took my breath away, and not only for their grandeur. The high winds that swept down from their pinnacles transformed the highway into a capricious funnel.

The first day's drive up to Laredo and then north to meet up with Route 10W was only the first act in the battle for road security. I soon forgot about the spiritual lessons of splendid isolation as I fought to keep the camper on the road. The Falcon was not at its best on long meandering upgrades. It met the challenge by steadily losing momentum and forcing us into the right-hand slow lane behind all the behemoth trucks.

"Come on, old friend," I shouted into the air. "You can do this! You *have* to do this!" Looking around at the wildly minimalist landscape of unrelieved browns and grays against a sky of vivid blue without a soul or town in sight, closed in by the unrelenting barrier of mountains that never seemed to come closer, I prayed that God and Nature were the same.

Go with it, breathe it in, become part of it, do not resist floated the words in my interior space. *Return to breathing; return to patterns of creation; return to life's stream; return to the power that is in all things.* Chanting these words of encouragement got us through to a campsite somewhere near Kerrville. It wasn't as far as I had hoped to go that day, but it was adequate for gathering strength for at least one more long distance drive through Texas. .

The second day made all my former windy experiences gentle puff balls by comparison. The sheer vastness of the uninterrupted high desert plains, sparsely littered with low vegetation, once again threatened to overwhelm my senses and clarified my own modest presence in the universe as somewhere among the grains of sand. As the day progressed, the winds buffeted the Falcon mercilessly. Very few other transports were on the highway, and those tended to be the huge semis that simply added to my feelings of fragility. If I passed them, I knew I was pushing the van to its upper limits; if they passed me, I was truly in danger of being blown out of my lane. I was so desperate that I tried the trick of staying in the draft of one to let it draw the Falcon and take the winds head-on to give me a break. This worked until the hated upgrades where the semis lost even more momentum than the Falcon and forced us to an almost standstill creep.

Once again, I sang every song and hymn I knew, starting with Gene Autry's *Tumbling Tumbleweed.* Everywhere I looked that weed was head over thorns, rolling, slipping, running with the wind at its back, racing across the rough plains determined to reach some invisible finish line known only to itself and Poseidon. I would have been laughing in delight if I were not using every molecule of energy I had holding the Falcon to the road.

My goal was to camp that night in the little corner of New Mexico that lies between it and Arizona. By mid-afternoon, and still hours from my goal, I was wrung out, dried up, and desperate for one of the elusive towns to appear on the horizon where I could pull off the road and into the first motel I came to. My existence reduced to extremely simplistic needs: to stop the pounding of the wind, to ease the rigid muscles in my upper body, and to find some congenial company.

I was desperate to talk to anybody, to reconnect this insignificant speck of dust to a sense of being human. I needed a place of belonging and identity. I felt like someone who had been rescued from a raft in the midst of a raging storm where all control had been stripped away and had lay bare my soul's longing for trust and hope. Relief washed over me when I drove the van into a motel parking lot, leaving me limp with the aftermath of spent adrenaline

A chattering, laughing group of fellow travelers were gathered around small tables in the lounge. A banked fire in the fieldstone fireplace pulled me, with its irresistible reminders of normalcy and home, into a room whose high windows looked out on a deserted patio. The surface of the water in the pool had whitecaps. The tables and chairs surrounding it were blown into positions for which they were never designed. Surreally, the sky was intensely calm and the sun so bright I felt like I had been plopped down in the middle of a play where I did not know the lines. The contrast between the inner and the outer could not have been greater.

"Guess we won't be enjoying the outdoor amenities of the place, will we?" asked one of the men comfortably lounging in a captain's chair near the fire.

"You don't go in the water unless its 75 degrees anyway," teased his wife. Turning to me she smiled an invitation to sit with them and several others who were kibitzing about the conditions on the road.

There was such relief in knowing that I wasn't the only one who had reached a limit. We shared food and coffee with that light feeling of gemutlicheit that comes when strangers are forced to seek temporary solace and safety in each others company. Someone shushed us as the TV news came on over the bar at the other end of the room.

The sensational item at the top of the hour was the high winds wreaking havoc all over the southwest. The camera zeroed in on a crumpled heap of whiteish metal at the bottom of a ravine. The newscaster's voice-over gave me chills.

"An RV has been swept off the road, broad sided by high winds. There is no word yet if there are any survivors. State Police are issuing a warning that recreational vehicles use extreme caution when attempting mountain passes, especially the smaller top-heavy ones." I closed my eyes when the broadcaster went on to say that this accident happened in *New Mexico,* and that several others had been reported as far away as northern Arizona. Southern Arizona was spared.

One more time I went to sleep thanking God for sending me to Tucson and not where my logic and controlling ego would have taken me. One more time I was grateful for listening to the inner voice and trusting it enough to act. Of course, I had no way of knowing that night how important Tucson would be and that I would break all records and remain there for over two months. In many ways it was the prize for endurance at the end of a marathon.

II
Tucson

Years ago when we lived in Arizona during my former husband's military obligation with the US Public Health Service, Tucson was one of our playgrounds. It was a place to go to get off the reservation for a much needed respite to shop at the BX on Davis Monthan Air Force Base, slip over the border into Nogales for great Mexican food, and swim with the children in a luxury motel made affordable by military rates. Usually we went to the more urban Phoenix for these same delights, but Tucson and its proximity to Mexico made it one of our special family outings.

Now, for some reason, I was going back to the Sonora desert to bear witness to the coming of spring to the earth and new creativity to my life. But I had to wonder if I were also tripping through another part of my past in order to provoke or heal another hole in my soul. I was achingly aware that in my younger life Arizona was one of the places where I had never said goodbye well. Though I cherished warm and transforming memories of our two years on an Apache reservation, I had not allowed myself to be invested in *leaving*. Those were the days I protected myself by focusing only on *going*. Was it now time to integrate this experience and change the outcome?

With memories of Apache camp dresses and massive flowering cacti after a spring rain floating in my head, I watched the skyline of Tucson come closer and realized that, once again, I had landed in a spot without any idea where to go. I passed campground after campground on the way into the city, but none of them were quite right.

Before I knew it, I had passed any chance of finding a place to park for the night and was navigating late afternoon city traffic right into the downtown melee of commuters blasting their way home. Ignoring all this, I was entranced with the cultural center that was nothing like the one I remembered from the late sixties. I knew down to my toenails that I wanted to be in a campground where I had access to this shining place. Museums, shops, university; I felt my psyche soar. Why this was so I had no idea. I only knew that the inner voice was calling out, *this is it!*

Finding a suitable campground took me several false starts until I took a hard look at what my resistance was to the natural ones in state or county parks, the ones that were tucked into mountains or in sheltered desert spaces, that offered nature walks and biking trails. This time I did not want to be out in the wilds of nature no matter how inspiring and beautiful. Barely understanding it myself, the only way I could describe what I needed was a place that was close to *intellectual* centers. So with mixed emotions and feeling something like a cop-out, I found an RV resort similar to the one in Texas that provided indoor-outdoor pools, clubhouse and activities.

Most of the people were repeat snowbirds who wintered there every year. I signed up for a month with slight trepidation. However, there was not a mention of anything remotely called a singles group. Things were truly looking up when no one told me about another single woman traveling to California towing a Mercedes.

I set up my campsite, complete with awning, picnic table and chairs and was just congratulating myself when a gust of wind swept through threatening the stability of the awning and I knew that I had been somewhat precipitous. It was only late February and the desert winds could still be capricious, especially in the late afternoon. The front office assured me that the area was just emerging from a cold snappy winter, but each day would be getting warmer. The crowd gathered around the outdoor pool appeared tanned and social. That augured well for relaxation when needed.

The whole climate was different from Outdoor Resorts. There were planned activities, but most of them were day trips or lectures. There were no weekly potlucks and dances, no organized group that went to local watering holes for entertainment, no coffee shop talk of war, and no clubby atmosphere for women to congregate and share their stories. In fact, for the first time on my journey, I was not treated as though I were an oddity that needed constant feeding and entertaining. People were friendly in that distant, "Hi, how are you?" way; but most everyone was part of a couple and had their social groups well intact. For some reason, this bothered me not at all. I smiled and made light conversation at the pool; but there was never any pressure to follow up.

The first morning I went to the door of my van and gazed out at the mountains ringing the desert to the north and to the moonscape garden that surrounded the resort. Lifting my coffee cup I toasted the heavens, blue beyond imagining, and gave thanks for the peacefulness that washed over me. I was feeling the bliss of unhurried Time, the sheer gift of a chance to reflect once again, and to examine the sense of lightness, of being exactly where I was supposed to be.

Over the next few days, I understood that Texas had been a rerun of that old dichotomy of the tug and tension between my *internal* world of spirit and creativity, and the social demands of my *external* world where I can so easily focus exclusively on people and activity. I sat outside in the lingering sun's descent, chuckling at this bit of self-knowledge, *Oh well, it only took you a little over a month this time, not fifty years*. That had to be some sort of positive maturity and maybe a wee tad of integration.

The desert began to work its dry, clean-air magic, blowing away the musty lingering webs of the previous month and a half. Christine came for a week and we played at being real tourists.

I rented a car and was surprised by how vulnerable I felt driving something so close to the road. We toured the area visiting the Desert Museum, Old Tucson Studios where so many of the classic westerns were filmed, Saguaro National Park, and of course, Nogales, Mexico. We called an old acquaintance from the East who invited us to have dinner in his parents' home where, for a little while, I could pretend that I lived just like everybody else.

The most dynamic gifts of having my friend with me were the intangibles of a multi-faceted feminine friendship. We lay in our beds at night laughingly sharing stories of her new marriage and my trip adventures. We chuckled over men and seriously dissected our insights about everything. This kind of friendship allows for deep, deep connection where isolation is only possible if it is self-imposed. My friend was the *Wise Woman* of myth and truth and song, allowing me to see myself as reflected in her eyes and heart, holding me accountable to my own visions and dreams and gracing me with the sagacity of her most loving reality check. We swung from giggling like teenagers to deep discussions of love and commitment, to drinking margaritas, to spiritual sharing, to the practicalities of living life as fully as possible on the proverbial shoestring.

She got serious for moment as she looked around my van, "You're really doing it, Jeanie. You're really living out your dream."

"I am," I repeated solemnly. "Some days I still can't quite believe it. But it's beginning to sink in. I'm really *here!*"

"Part of me envies you, you know. This is something we used to talk about doing together." There was honest conflict in her eyes.

"I know. But, hey, you decided that marriage and Marc were more important than a camping trip. What can I say?" I joked.

"Oh my God, what's wrong with me? I just want it all!" She threw her hands extravagantly in the air as we both burst out laughing at this old refrain repeated frequently through the years. She was so profoundly right. We do want it all. We want deeply satisfying relationships with profound intimacy and creativity. We want self-knowledge that is born out of deep reflection and experience of the spiritual connectedness to the Giver of Life. Naturally, we want comfort and security and time to enjoy all the pleasures that grow out of each and every sincere encounter with truth and love. Of course we want it all. The trick is in learning what *all* is.

I kept the car for a few more days after Chris left, taking advantage of the mobility to go farther afield to Benson. I wasn't quite ready to go back to my self-imposed isolation. I was yet ruminating over all the joys of the past week. The side trip enchanted with the surprising active and thriving art colonies of southern Arizona. I promised myself that I would get back for more.

In Tombstone I witnessed the ongoing shoot-out at OK Corral and walked into the old saloon in the town "too tough to die." I even ate lunch in the hotel dining room where, a sign assured me, Wyatt Earp ate his noontime meal. How my Dad would have enjoyed this walk into history. I had to laugh thinking about that contradictory pacifist minister who loved nothing better than a shoot-em-up western on Saturday afternoons after his sermon was written. Was that having it all, too?

Winter was fast becoming spring and my trip was at the half-way mark. The time had come for me to intentionally seek the rhythm of silence once again and to listen for directions, to figure out what it was that I was drawn to here in Tucson.

My daily meditative walks in the large resort pulled me to the outlying row of parked RV's and human habitation. One step more would thrust me beyond the bounds of civilization into the wilderness of open spaces relieved only by cacti and moonscape rocks. Occasionally I caught a glimpse of diving hawks and scary, crawly unfamiliar life forms. It was not unlike standing at the edge of the ocean so many times last fall, awed by the sheer force and power in front of me which could so easily overwhelm and dominate.

Not for the first time I reminded myself that this desert, too, had once been ocean. I could stand on my tiptoes at the sandy edge of all that was familiar and struggle with my fear of taking the next step, as I had done so many times before. If I had the courage, I could plunge into the land of the unknown. Like the Apaches I had once lived among, I could hold out my arms, open my heart and greet the Great Spirit who would enhance my vision and teach me to sing the stories of my people and my life.

Chapter 17
From Sunrise to God's Eye

The desert ever enchants with its changing colors of springtime, and with the daily drama of watching the sun shoot its colors across the sky at dawn and dusk. The vastness is like the ocean—immutable, flowing and ever mesmerizing. The mountains are just as present—hovering around the city—always close—always distant—ever changing, ever still. Everyday I think "I will lift up mine eyes unto the hills from whence cometh my help..." The same words that graced my days wherever I have lived and have been given a sense of being home.
  Journal: Tucson, February

I
Inside Threads

A certain woman in the Old Testament took up residence in my psyche, perching there with foot-swinging aplomb, implacably awaiting my attention. Sloe-eyed and sleek this ancient wife of little known historical fact or reputation seemed to be demanding that I tell her story. The idea of writing a novel had been germinating for weeks, but I was in no hurry to pay it any attention. I was at long last in the midst of writing a non-fiction book on women's spirituality, using the lives of several Marys of the New Testament as my voice. What right did this ancient woman have, pushing her way into my consciousness when I clearly did not have time for her? But push she did.

By the strangest phenomenon, the more time I spent contemplating the desert, the more she made herself at home. The more I struggled with the underlying meaning and reasoning for my being in Tucson, the more real she became. Before I fell asleep at night, I found myself asking who she was. When I contemplated the desert terrain on my morning walks I wondered what her life was like. What was the climate of her time, who was in power, what place in her world would a woman of her status enjoy? I would read the paper and end up wondering what were the political, social and economic ramifications of the reigning power in her world? As I wrote from the time of modernity, I pondered on what were the varieties of religious movements in her day and how did they affect her and those around her? More importantly for me, how was I to learn any of this living in a van on the western side of the city of Tucson, Arizona, 3000 plus years in her future?

In the end, it was quite simple. Access to the university was one of the attractions that had originally excited me about parking the Falcon where it was. I headed for the university and the research library with some trepidation about a non-student being allowed into its sacred stacks.

"Excuse me," I approached the research librarian behind the very effective barrier counter. "I'm a temporary resident here and would like to do some research for a book I am writing." The slight exaggeration only bothered my conscience for a second. I was, truthfully, writing a book, just not the one I was desperate to research.

"Of course," she blandly acquiesced, throwing me completely off balance. Of course? This would not happen at Harvard. Was this one of the differences between a state and a private institution? My eyes narrowed.

"What is the fee for this service?" I challenged.

"No fee," she smiled while she hauled out a few papers. "But you will have to fill out this form if you want an ID card to come and go more easily."

While I completed the form, she informed me of the rules. "...and you must conduct all your research in the library. No books may be removed. You can, however, use the copy machines to run-off anything pertinent and observe all copyright laws in your publication." I was mesmerized. She was taking me seriously. My thanks were heartfelt beyond anything her programmed words deserved. She believed me when I said I was a writer. Or maybe, I was beginning to believe myself.

"Oh, yes," I turned back to the desk, "where will I find the Ancient History section?"

She smiled wholeheartedly and pointed to the elevator. "What a refreshing question! Hardly anyone goes up there anymore. Mostly IT these days. At least you won't have to wait for someone to return the sources you need." We both chuckled at the absurdity of there being a rush on ancient history.

I can still see the desk I staked out for the duration, where it fit in the library, up high under a window away from most of the grad students writing their theses and dissertations. I was a bit self-conscious about being so much older and a bit of a fraud amidst all that high academic achievement. I needn't have worried about being asked to defend my thesis. The librarian was right. There weren't many students wallowing in the wars of Phoenicia, Assyria, Babylon, Egypt and Persia. In fact, most of the students came to the AH section to privately and illegally use their cell phones.

I was the only one carrying piles of books juxtaposing the rise of civilizations and religious monotheism, as well as anything I could find on the ancient diasporas of the Jews. Nor did anyone wait impatiently while I detoured for hours over *A Day in the Life of Babylon.* This was all new territory for me and I discovered a deep and abiding love for pouring over manuscripts that transported me into another time and place. I savored the musty smells of old books mingled with waxed wood worn down over time, breathing in their rare perfume as though by doing so I could effortlessly be filled with all their collective knowledge. Is this how people write novels, I wondered? If so, how do you know when your research is finished? There's always something more to discover about another age.

It felt so satisfying to go *home* at the end of the day, tired but replete with accomplishment. I stood at the edge of the undulating oceanic desert and closed my eyes in gratitude and thanksgiving for the peace in my soul. My Lady of the Old Testament desert danced behind my eyelids, a slow ritual to the closing of the day. The sounds of lute and drum introduced the chanting of the singer in the shadows. And then I knew why this woman felt so familiar. I had seen her as a girl not in the deserts of ancient times but right here in my time. I had seen her as an Apache girl-child dancing her way to maturity not at sunset but at sunrise.

One of the first invitations my husband and I received when we moved to the reservation all those years ago with two small babes came from another doctor's wife. We had only been in residence a couple of weeks, still wondering if we would ever adjust to the dry, dusty, barren desert with July temperatures over 110 degrees. The kids were cranky from staying indoors, and I was bored by the lack of anything that looked like adult social interaction. Kay came calling with her two children and a thermos of icy piquant homemade lemonade. That day I had my first drink of the reservation's community spirit.

"Of course the kids play outside," she assured me with a tiny hint of condescension. "You just want to keep them in during the hottest part." I asked her about where to buy sand for a sandbox, and she rolled her eyes. "You sure are from back East. Sticks out a mile." This was the first time I had ever heard anyone say *back east* in the same tones I had heard in my childhood about *up north*. Her honest laughter took away any meanness of the words to a perceived eastern city slicker.

"I think we can find you some sand around here," she looked meaningfully out the window at the earth's bountiful sandbox. "But if you want to pay for some, I guess we could find you a store somewhere."

For some reason, despite my southern-northern-eastern naiveté, Kay adopted me. She and her husband were from Oklahoma and he was part Native American. Their guidance and introduction to southwestern culture were invaluable. It was because of their acceptance in the Native population that Kay called me one day with an invitation.

"We want you and Jim to come to a Sunrise Dance with us this weekend." I had no idea what she was talking about. "We've arranged for a sitter for you, 'cause we have to be out by the mesa before sunrise, about 4 o'clock in the morning." I was intrigued but hated to let her know that once again I was lost. "This is real important, you know. My husband knows the father. White people usually aren't invited to the sacred ceremonies. But this is sort of like a debutante's coming-out. Traditionally her family provides all the food and gifts and everyone gathers around while she dances as the sun comes up. These days the families are too poor, so everyone pitches in. We think you'll like it."

It was so dark that the cars had to park in a circle with their lights on while everything was set up. Campfires were in the distance and their smoke bore testimony to the pots of food cooking for the daylong party to come. We stood in the predawn chill feeling time out of mind.

The drums started their beat, sending chills up my spine as every preconceived stereotype of Apaches danced in my head. Women, in colorful traditional camp dresses proudly displaying ornate silver squash blossom necklaces and complicated bead work, mingled with men in jeans and western shirts sporting huge silver and turquoise buckles. Children in buckskins and camp dresses darted in and out testing the limits as all children do. The atmosphere was somber as the crowd banked the sides of a long display of food and gifts set out on woven blankets.

A hush fell as the car lights blinked out and we could see the forms taking shape out of the dense darkness. A voice rang out, chanting in Apache, which at first was disconcerting. I wanted to know what he was saying. But as the chant went on, it ceased to matter. Minute by minute the scene was getting lighter and clearer. Then the singer stopped. There was only the silence of the desert and the held breaths of dozens of people as we waited together for what was about to commence.

A young girl stepped into place at the head of the offerings so carefully placed on the blankets. She was dressed in beaded buckskins and around her head was a band with a silver medallion in the middle of her forehead. Her feet were wrapped in suede fringed boots and decorated with silver bells. Next to her was another girl dressed the same, without the headband. They stood straight and silent staring off into the stark distance at the mesa dead ahead and miles away. To the side were several men with drums and one elderly man who seemed to be in charge. The anticipation was building within the group. What was going on? What were we waiting for? The girls were uncannily still and expectant. Centered, waiting, ancient and beautiful.

Then the elderly man began to sing again. And as he sang the girls slowly started to stamp their feet to the rhythm. Slowly, slowly, their ankle bells faintly carried on the early desert breeze. Almost imperceptibly they all began to add to the pace. And suddenly, as though conjured by the magic of the music and the beauty of the girls, the first pink streaks were seen on the horizon backlighting the mesa. The girls whirled dance after dance celebrating the rising of the sun and the new day's dawning of adulthood. The old singer pointed to the south, the north, the east and the west. Instinctively I knew he was calling upon all the universe to bear witness to the coming of this day. As the sun rose, the desert got hotter and hotter. Still they danced on, seemingly oblivious to the brightness and the heat, ever staring into the sun over the far mesa. Finally, they stopped. We shook ourselves from the trancelike state, drank water and waited for what was next when the drums took up again.

Quietly and quickly, the companion dancer melted away as the symbol of leaving childhood behind. Then in a dramatic moment the young woman fell on her face, spread-eagled on the sand while a group of older women, in their long dresses, danced around her. Eventually, they, too, wandered away leaving only the grandmother to lean over as she step-danced, laying her hands on the supine form, molding the body of the young girl coming of age from childhood into womanhood.

I did not need to understand Apache after all. The symbol acted out in front of me touched a place in me that was universal. She was becoming a woman, accepted into the community as a woman, blessed by the Great Spirit through the singing of the men and the beat of the drum, and by the elder women who paved her way. What woman among us could watch and not know, not be blessed by the truth that down deep in the feminine we are all part of the same mystery?

It took a trip to Tucson to remember all of this at the end of the day while watching streaks of deep apricot and gold light the sky before slipping away into the lavenders and purples of night. In that breathless moment of recognition, my Old Testament Woman, connected by her desert life in ancient times to the desert life of women here and now, danced forward and joined hands making me the link between.

The coming of aging, I ruminated, was to be able to see the big picture. If we look, we begin to see all of the sun's journey from its rising in the east of childhood when everything was an enchantment and so new to the self. We begin to remember standing in the blinding noonday light of youthful dreams, without shadows to obfuscate the external landscape, when we *knew* we saw it all. The cooling down of the late afternoon of mid-life is when we start to get glimpses that we are changing as the day marches on. Then the peacefulness of early evening calls us to sit for a moment and to reflect on the internal landscape of the day and to wonder about our tomorrows. And finally, we are in the setting sun, looking back at our world, our lifetime, being conscious enough to give back what we have learned; to step-dance around the bodies of our young and stretch out our hands with song, prayer and wisdom to pass it along. What a legacy! And I wondered, as I stood there on the edge of the Tucson desert, if there were any ceremony or ritual for passing into the evening of aging?

II
Outside Threads

Eventually, my extroverted nature demanded that I get out and meet people. A friend of a friend from *back east* invited me to his home for a dinner party that turned out to have unexpected consequences.

We were an intergenerational group with professions ranging from left brain engineers to right brain artists, from college mathematics professor to at least two psychotherapists. Two were retired and a lively discussion ensued about whether or not *I* was as well. *That was a breezy dismissal of my sabbatical,* I thought. It threatened me with an unwelcome identity. The professor said that I couldn't link my sabbatical directly to my work, that research for an historical novel had no bearing on my field for either greater insight or for practical remuneration. Therefore, I wasn't on a sabbatical.

His words cut to my deepest insecurity that I was wasting time by not utilizing my psychotherapy experience. I had no defense against his reasoning. When I hinted that I was on a spiritual journey, perhaps led by deep intuition or divine energy, the conversation thankfully shot into other waters. Everybody weighed in with a lively opinion about the spiritual life, and some were vulnerable enough to share their sacred experiences. I even tried to explain how my spiritual life informed my work as a psychotherapist, especially in the worlds of recovery, reconciliation, death and grief. Not wanting to risk further comment by the erudite professor, I used Carl Jung as my reference, not Jesus, Mother Theresa or Meister Eckhart.

By dessert, we were onto politics. By coffee, we were talking about the mellow mundane: the joys of a southwestern lifestyle. At the end of the evening, several people suggested *great* singles groups they were active in. Two days later, I had a message taped to the Falcon asking me to call a woman I had met at the party.

"I have a guest house that is empty at the moment. It is semi-detached from the house and the studio. Would you be interested in using it while you are here?" The offer came totally unexpectedly. I had made no plans for such a contingency in this year of living frugally in the Falcon. A move such as this would change the quality and perspective of my journey in ways I couldn't begin to imagine on the phone.

"I wasn't asking for rent," she explained, "just for a small amount of your time." She went on to explain that she had listened closely to what I said at the dinner party and knew that she wanted to work with me. I quickly explained about boundaries, client-therapist relationship, licensure and all of the myriad potential problems living in close proximity could produce.

"I'm not talking about doing therapy," she explained. "I already have that resource. I need something else from you, but I hate talking about personal matters over the phone." Intrigued, I agreed to meet her for lunch in her home and hear her story. I went, however, seriously doubting that I wanted to give up my freedom and autonomy by moving out of the Falcon.

She was very persuasive. Entering her seventies, she wanted to grieve the loss of a beloved one and reconcile with the passing of time and some physical problems caused by the onset of aging.

"I'm afraid I have worn out my family and overburdened my friends," she laughed. She zeroed in on my eyes, "Can you believe I have reached the point where I read the obits every morning before I even read the editorials?" I certainly would not have pegged her as one who was losing heart, I told her. She looked and acted at least ten to fifteen years younger than her age.

"That's the point," she said. "I look younger, but I no longer *feel* younger. Like an old woman, I can't seem to stop talking about my beloved, telling the same stories over and over. Like I can't get enough of hearing about him myself. Everyone, including my *therapist,*" she threw out ironically, "tells me to get on with my life. Well, I am. I work, I produce, I make a good income. I see my family, play with the grandkids, travel. But I need to move on in some way I can't describe. The way you have."

That threw me. The way I have? Is that how she perceived me? I must have looked perplexed. Selfishly, all I could focus on was that I was twenty years younger, but she saw me as a contemporary.

Impatiently she said, "Your talk the other night, about intuition, about the deep sense of dependence on the creative. The divine. Was all that talk about living from the inside out just smoke?" I shook my head. "Well, what I would like from you is your skill and experience in bereavement and lessons about the coming of aging." I was stunned. What an idea. Could it work? How would we work out the practical terms starting with time limits, boundaries, and autonomy? Was I ready to share with anyone what I was still in the midst of myself?

I could hear the quiver of fear in my voice when I begged for time. I needed to integrate and process her wild idea. I needed to get back to the campground resort and dive into the depths of meditation and prayer. I needed to listen in silence to the inner voice. Free rent in exchange for being a confidant and friend to a glorious woman I call

"Gloria," who could allow her to tell her stories, be in the present with her feelings, and have discussions about what I was learning. At the same time, I had to be free to continue my research at the University of Arizona. There was an Iranian professor who had agreed to meet with me and give me pointers about the ancient middle-east, the role of women, extant poetry and other primary sources. I couldn't give that up.

Gloria was not only persuasive, she was canny. After lunch, she showed me through the rest of her adobe southwestern home decorated in earth tones and filled with original art work by local artists. The most original, however, were the heart-stopping vistas emanating in all directions and beautifully framed by tall, clear windows. She took me through her studio and introduced me to family and younger artists she mentored. And finally, the semi-detached guest house with complete kitchen, real beds, and my most favorite therapy: a bathtub slanted perfectly for reclining and reading. Unfair tactics.

Wasn't this trip about doing a new thing, breaking out of the mold of external expectations and daring to risk being different on the inside? The words echoed and re-echoed until I began to pay attention. Letting go of orthodoxy and being present in a new way was an exciting supposition. *This is all learning as both teacher and pupil. Gloria has much to teach you as well.*

Synchronistically, my month was almost up at the Resort; it was time to either reregister or move on to other places. No inner stirrings or voice were telling me to leave Tucson. Not only was I writing well on my book, but I was also deeply involved in the convenience of getting to know the ancient world. There were several new acquaintances that kept me in their loop of get-togethers. I was settling into a newfound rhythm of daily living that satisfyingly plugged some more of those holes in my soul.

Without fanfare, I drove my Falcon to the house, and for the first time in seven months emptied its insides into a place with real room. Nothing had to be bungeed down. The computer could remain set up until I left. My clothes could be hung in a closet wrinkle free. I could buy enough food for a week and know the frig was large enough to store it, and I could sink down into a bubble bath anytime I wished. Oh the pleasures I had taken for granted all my life!

My new friend and I had a contractual agreement beneficial to both of us. She and I met formally twice a week at designated times for a specified length of time. Any other exchanges were social and were to be agreed upon, such as sharing a meal, or going out. Rules of confidentiality applied, as well as rules of respecting one another's privacy. There could be no popping in to each other's space. And most importantly, we would not pick up on the conversations held in our formal times during our informal times.

She was busy, and so, surprisingly, was I. Yet I was always aware of the constant swirl of creativity going on next door. The air was heavy with it, seeping into my side of the property, enticing me ever deeper into its flow. *What a gift*, I thought, *to be surrounded by people whose talent and focus were to expose life as metaphor, as a moment, captured in the instant of a hawk's wings, a clay pot, a painting, or a piece of metal stretched into a thousand shapes.*

Other than the art, the greatest gift I grabbed with heart and soul was the matter-of-fact simplicity with which the artists accepted the strivings of others. No defense of sabbaticals was required. It was tacitly understood that whatever one has to do to support the inner driving passion to take what is on the inside and give it form on the outside is perfectly acceptable. That was virgin territory to one who had thought all her life that such stirrings were at best a cultured pastime or at worst distractions from taking life seriously.

One more time, over the ensuing weeks, I experienced the soul moving preciousness of walking with another through the deepest part of grief and reconciliation. There was never a moment that I was not aware of how sacred was our dance together over holy ground. Gloria's grief was also my grief, as is the way of the human condition. When I held her stories, her words and her tears, they washed over me in my innermost heart and bathed me once again in the purifying ritual of coming to terms with my own memories of grief and loss. This gathering of the pieces of brokenness in our souls connected us to one another, strangers or friends, with binding threads of our shared humanity. "Why," I wrote in my journal, "are we humans so careless of being authentically present and truthful one to another? Do we not take the time, or are we so profoundly mistrustful of our own inner feelings, so frightened at what might be unleashed, that we take refuge in platitudes, denial and advice giving?"

Recalling the woman I met in Africa who had so much to say about the differences in our cultures, I wished with all my heart she were there in Tucson. I wanted her to know that understanding was dawning, and that African village life was being played out in some sense in Arizona. The real work of being human was to listen with empathy and compassion to each others stories. That sharing creativity in all of its myriad manifestations was the voice of the divine speaking through each one of us. And that wisdom, compassion and empathy are the products of being aware of our shared humanity. I was not only passing along to Gloria what I was learning about living from the inside out, she was giving me a glorious glimpse into the daily realities of the next stage of the coming of aging.

March melded into April and income taxes loomed. One can go, leave, run, or stay, it makes no difference to the federal government. Gloria sent me to her accountant who helped me work through the maze of living on the road while owning a house in Massachusetts. Putting everything together, filing and waiting for the return took time. Enormously relieved of the burden of deciding whether or not it was time to move on, I happily continued wallowing in Gloria's hospitality, working up a sweat in the increasingly hot air, working on my several writing and research projects, and being entertained by the various people I met. In other words, I was settling in, or down, or whatever the euphemism is for becoming part of a community.

III
To God's Eye

When my modest check came from the government, I knew I would no longer have any excuse to remain in Tucson. One of my only preplanned destinations for the whole trip was to be in California when my brother finished teaching for the year. That time was fast approaching and I had so much yet to see. And do. And be. In my mother's words, my feet were getting itchy.

Gloria's grief was noticeably less raw. There were fewer tears and much more laughter in her recollections of her beloved. She was also far more focused on needing to finish her commissions, some family issues, and an upcoming trip. We had mapped out her goals for her immediate life, and achievable goals for the long term. She had gone beyond mere acceptance to *living with* her realities, even to rediscovering the nascent tips of new growth poking their heads through the ground of her being. Reconciliation. A time to integrate her life before her loss into who she was now, a woman tempered by experience, made more whole by the 'slings and arrows' inevitable to all of us. And I hope she learned that she needed to stretch out and ask for the kind of support she needed from family and friends. (A reminder to myself, as well.)

So it was on April 30th that I took one more day to revisit some of my favorite spots in Tucson. I headed out about 9AM for one of the upscale malls tucked up on the foothills overlooking the city. I wasn't going there to shop, I was going there to see original art. Tucson's art museum had a program of taking art to the people, their theory being that if large numbers of people won't come to the art exhibits in the museum, they would take the art to them in the malls. Lovely.

I was too early. The metal gate was firmly locked; no lights anywhere. Something caught my eye in the store window next door. A stunning display of handmade Native American jewelry was spread out on velvet, catching the light of the display case and pulling me into its orbit. It was one of those moments, rare for me, when I *wanted*. I *coveted* so intensely that I had to put my hands behind my back, fearing I might claw through the glass. Those rings, necklaces, bracelets and brooches conjured up sunrise dances, sunsets, Apaches, drums, medicine songs, wickiups, and barren mesas. Something ancient was calling out to my blood. The intricate workings in silver and turquoise, inlaid corral, lapis, and malachite worked on my senses. Their original designs were hard to define, not quite traditional, yet not quite postmodern. Someone was a true artiste, for each piece was made with love. I just knew it. And far, far beyond my tax rebate. It was truly one of those embarrassing moments when I regretted not being a doctor's wife anymore. Then I was ashamed of myself for what that implied.

There was someone standing next to me. How long had she been there? How long had I been there? I glanced over and beheld a petite Native American woman with graying black hair sleeked back in the traditional bun. Tiny and wrinkled and somewhat stooped, she was as still and silent as a ghost, clutching her overlarge sweater across her chest while staring just as intently at the jewelry as I.

Slightly unnerved, although if anyone had asked I wouldn't have been able to say why, I shifted my stance and went back to silently watching the prizes dancing out of reach behind the glass. Finally, as is so typical of white people in social situations, I broke the silence.

"It's beautiful," I said pointing to the display, "isn't it?" She shifted slightly, barely nodding her head. A few more seconds go by while my discomfort increases. Maybe she hated seeing her people's work sold in designer jewelry stores owned by white people who were not known for generously sharing their profits with the artists.

"I love those designs." slipped unguarded past my lips. Darn! Maybe she was one of the *old ones* who hated seeing their traditional jewelry patterns replaced by upstart designs which pander to the commercial world. Her silence was definitely putting me on the defensive. After a few more moments of uncomfortable quiet, came words that rocked my world.

"What do you see?" came the low voice. My heart skipped a beat at that so- familiar inner-voice question. I started to turn to her in surprise. *"Look around you,"* she repeated, *"and what do you see?"* Her hand waved at the window forcing me to turn back to the jewelry.

"I -I see beauty that takes my breath away," I stuttered. "I see designs that are so original that I have not seen anything like them in all my travels. They are truly magnificent," I finished lamely, fancifully wondering if I were speaking to one of God's messengers

Then she nodded. A brief smile lit her tiny face while she looked me in the eye. "Oh, so you have some of *our* jewelry? she asked somewhat skeptically I thought.

"Not from this artist," I assured her. "Years ago we lived on one of the Apache reservations. I have a few pieces from that time." Her gaze narrowed. "Then later when we were visiting family in New Mexico I bought a Singer necklace that I enjoy wearing."

"Navajo," she confirmed. I nodded not knowing where to go next. "San Carlos?" she asked. Again I nodded too surprised to form words. How did she know?

"My husband was working in the hospital there," I sort of blurt.

"Did you know Sadie?" she asked me out of the blue.

Now I am really blown apart. I turned to her. "Do you know Sadie? The nurse in the hospital? She had an adorable little girl...Oh; I can't remember her name..."

In the midst of my stumbling over my tongue, she quietly said. "We dance together, her people and my people. Sadie's little girl is now a mother herself. We meet, we dance several times a year. These are good people."

Sadly, I say another little goodbye to my past, for Sadie and her little one were forever locked in my memory as young. Quietly I shared with the old woman some of my feelings about the time I lived among the Apaches, but never one of them until the last night before we left and Sadie showed up at the door. When I asked her to come in, she shyly declined and pulled something out from behind her back and thrust it into my hands.

"Here," she said, "I want you to have this. It was my grandmother's."

I looked down at the soft, worn, beaded buckskin bag dangling from my fingers. "Oh, Sadie, thank you! Are you sure you want to let this out of your family?"

She smiled as she walked away. "It's not going out of my family."

As I recounted this to the old woman, I felt the tears begin at the back of my eyes. "That purse is on the wall of every house I have lived in since we left San Carlos. And so is the cradleboard. I cannot forget the richness of that time there." I turned back to the window so as not to have to look her in the eyes. We stood companionably for a few minutes. Then she touched my arm.

"Come with me out to my car in the parking lot." She turned toward the door leading to the outside.

Nervously, I followed behind, somewhat uncomfortable with this turn of events. As if sensing my uncertainty, she beckoned me forward. We stopped behind an old Ford sedan and she opened the trunk. Jewelry cases were piled inside, dozens of them. She lifted a lid and there were several pieces obviously made by the same person as the ones in the window. I looked at her stupefied.

"My son and I make all those pieces you liked so well," she airily dismissed my incredulity as though her artistry were insignificant. She continued to hunt among the boxes until she said, "Ah, here it is!" and triumphantly turned toward me. In her hand was a simple silver ring topped by a deep green malachite stone surrounded by a silver collar. Definitely not as flashy as the rings inside the store. But not exactly traditional either with feathers and other designs worked into the silver. It was plain and beautiful and looked somewhat old.

"Here," she said as she handed it to me. "You are supposed to have this."

Still not getting the message, I regretfully told her that I couldn't afford one of their rings right now. She shook her head sadly, "This is not for money, this is a God's Eye, meant for you."

"For me?" Totally bewildered, I allowed her to place the ring on my palm and I looked closely. There embedded in the green stone, when I looked in the right light, I could see the dark circle that indeed looked like an eye. It followed me as I turned it this way and that. I didn't know what to say. I looked up at her serene face and knew that I must simply say, "Thank you." For this was truly a gift beyond price.

"Someday, I knew someone would come for the God's Eye. Remember to look around you and see what is here." With that, she was gone. Her part in this other-worldly little drama over, complete, finished. While I was left like a puppet, hand outstretched, holding a ring, waiting for the next pull of the string.

I slid the green stone on my left hand, ringless and bare for the past few years, and felt the solidity and comfort of its belonging there; coming home. Thrilled and dumbfounded, full of swirling feelings beyond naming, I climbed into the van with a strange sense of completeness. The older woman in my circle of humanity had danced into my life that day and passed something precious on to me. I had been searching for a ritual and it had found me in the foothills overlooking the desert I had grown to love.

The moment felt like another gestalt, that rare intensity when all things come together and settle in the soul with a sense of rightness. Once again, something indefinable in me had shifted. I was not only complete, I was replete. I could leave Tucson with tangible proof of grace and assurance that God's Eye was on me at all times.

Chapter 18
Backtracking

The road was new to me, as roads always are, going back.
Sarah Orne Jewett
The Country of the Pointed Firs
1896 Chapter 5

May in Arizona is August in New England. With the advent of serious heat, I became impatient with having to abandon the out-of-doors to seek out cool interiors for comfort. The city and all its energies had been a deeply satisfying break from living in more primitive parks and resort areas. The malls and restaurants which had satisfied my need for urban renewal were now beginning to pall. This was, after all, not my city, not my place of residence and work.

I had begun that insidious slide into the dangerous territory of *wanting* things, or *needing* things, as I circled through those places of commerce. I wrote in my journal, "It takes not only more energy to live here [city], but more vapid unthinking acquisition." The day I rationalized buying an extraordinarily lovely piece of wearable art I knew it was time to start listening, to plan for moving on. All the money I had saved on rent was going onto my bookshelves and on my back.

My reference library had grown commensurately as well. There was not a used bookshop in the city that I did not know intimately. I found a copy of the Whilhelm-Bryans edition of the *I Ching* as well as a study guide. These would enhance my inside-out listening skills, I hoped. A book of *Persian Wisdom,* sayings from the Avesta of ancient times, and *The Timetables of History: A Horizontal Linkage of People and Events* would allow me to continue my reading and research into ancient civilizations anywhere. The *New Larousse Encyclopedia of Mythology* and an old Reader's Digest copy of show and pop tunes were added one day because they were just so ridiculously cheap. I needed to get out of Arizona before I had to either rent a storage unit or start shipping stuff back home.

Tucson had given me the gift of time and space to write and create extensively. It had pointed the way to a deeper shift in my inner self away from my identity as a therapist toward the beginning of new ways in which to identify myself. None of this was concrete at that juncture, but the rise of something new, something creative, was starting, as it so frequently does, with a new restlessness in my soul. It was time to listen, trust and act once again and drive on to the next destination.

Saying goodbye well was important with Gloria, for we had shared so much about loss and leaving. We had both known from the outset that the final day was coming, that I had commitments to myself to honor by finishing my journey. One of the young artists made me a petroglyph of Kokopelli[12] carved into a chunk of red sandstone rock. It was a token of remembrance of my time among the artists who faithfully preserve the artistry of the ancient peoples who thrived in the canyons and pueblos long before our time.

The last two weeks in Tucson I deliberately slowed my pace, disengaged from social activities and prepared myself for the last stages of my trip. I wrote, I walked, I meditated, I said goodbye to those whose presence had fed my soul. And then I heard the intuitive nudge from the inner voice: *Now is the time to go to New Mexico.* That brought a chuckle, for if there is anything I am not good at, it is backtracking.

I

Albuquerque

It was a long, long day's drive to New Mexico from Tucson. The day, I think, was perfect: sunny, crisp, low wind, and absolutely stunning terrain. All of which passed through my consciousness with about as much awareness as sand slipping through the tube of the hour glass. Perhaps my psyche was on southwestern overload. More likely, I was in denial about needing to face a pertinent issue I avoided thinking about for months.

My former in-laws retired to a small town south of Albuquerque two decades previously. Our family had visited them over the years, so I was somewhat familiar with the area. Their son's divorce was a painful stigma for them to handle. There had been no closure between us. That whole long day, my internal debate about calling my children's grandparents precluded my seeing anything of the country I was passing through. When I stopped for gas at 4:30 PM, I took a deep breath, reminded myself that I was not the same person they had known, and called their house. After flabbergasted words of surprise, they invited me to stop by that evening. All I had to do was find a place for the night. They pointedly did not ask me to stay with them in the home where I had been so welcome for twenty years; another pesky pain under my sternum.

There was a motel on the secondary highway that passed their neighborhood development, family owned, clean and retro. The price was right, it was close, and I would only be there to sleep for a few hours before departing for Albuquerque the next day. If the parking lot was not buzzing with commerce, I barely noticed. What I did register subliminally was the gardener working just outside the office door. Something about the way he looked at me gave me a momentary shiver that I quickly passed off as I found the key to my room. I had other things to worry about, such as what on earth I was going to say to the intimate strangers I once shared a family with.

They had been in my life since I was nineteen, yet when we needed one another we had not been able to find a way to communicate. I knew they were shamed by the divorce; but I was puzzled by how it had become about them, not about what was happening to their son's family. Yet I knew as surely as I stood on the gold shag rug in that motel room that I harbored no ill will. I simply needed to see them, to have an authentic moment, then let it go. Surely, they too must have questions about the kids. Maybe our meeting would open doors for them to re-establish dialogue, or at least Christmas cards.

Their adobe house was as charming as ever. Dad still bragged about being smart enough to move to a place where there was no grass to cut, pointing as always with pride to his stone and cactus yard. The interior as well was eerily unchanged, suspending me for a nanosecond in a past where my husband or kids would come charging down the hall.

We sat formally in the living room, not around the kitchen table as we would have previously. *How sad,* I thought, *that we are reduced to this superficial act of entertaining.* I sat across the room from them trying to adjust to this new way of being. This was the woman who had passed on to me the sacrosanct recipes of the family's Hungarian foods, who poured out her heart to me about *her* mother-in-law problems, and who asked me to help her when she was having difficulty with a younger son. These are the people who were in my life for weddings, births, baptisms, holidays, the funerals of their parents, and endless other historic moments too dense to recall.

I set my coffee cup on the raised hearth next to the same awful gaudy gilt vase with the red and gold plastic flowers that my husband and I used to roll our eyes over in the privacy of the guest bedroom. And for one tiny second I had a poignant moment, one of those automatic married responses when I couldn't wait to share with him that his mom hadn't changed her décor in all this time.

They had aged since I had seen them last. Mom's back problems and Dad's heart by-pass had replaced the younger grandparents with white hair and stooped shoulders. Dad could barely look at me, while Mom smiled her small Christian good-girl smile. I dived right in and told them about my trip and why I was doing it. I spared them nothing of my body, mind and spirit.

Dad's eyes filled with tears. "We haven't known what to say to you."

"You should have called us more, Jeanie," mom added. "We were so ashamed of the divorce. But you should have called us more," she chastised ever so politely as she righteously added, "And we never heard from the kids."

I tried to laugh off this last comment by telling her that I didn't hear from them all that frequently either. I was having more difficulty laughing off their abdication of any responsibility in our mutual relationship, or for reaching out in love to their grandchildren.

"I did call you," I reminded them. "I was hurt and angry and your son was the cause. I didn't feel that it was fair to you to call and rant about him. No matter what had happened he was still your son. I just didn't have enough left in me to take care of your hurts, too. I'm so sorry."

They both looked contrite. But. Nothing more was said.

We spent the rest of the time catching up about families, just as though we were acquaintances who had come together for a short time after a long absence. *This, I thought later, is exactly what we were.* There was no sense of shared history in that house. No funny or silly anecdotes about their remembrances of the kids, no stories about *when* nor sighs of regret at time passing. More importantly, no burning questions about their grandchildren, or quest for current pictures. All was stately, cold and dead in that house. Or, I was dead in that house.

They walked me to the door, thanking me politely for stopping by, just as if I lived the next street over. Mom handed me a small glass jar layered with pretty stones and capped with a piece of cloth and a ribbon around it. On the side was taped a verse from the bible about rocks and sand and building houses.

"Here," she said taking my hand and placing the jar in it. "I pray this brings you comfort and joy." Getting downright chummy, she added, "Our women's group at church makes them for people who are going through, you know, what's the word? Crisis?" I stared at her. Then, I smiled politely and thanked her for her thoughtfulness. They waved me out of the driveway before they quickly turned back into their nice adobe house with the plastic flowers.

Oddly, I felt relieved, lighter, happy. She and her husband and their son were the sand upon which, as a young woman, I had built my house. Time and winds had washed it away. Now I was on a journey to find the rock upon which to build a new house. Yay! I zipped across the highway where a motel room awaited with popcorn, diet coke and a juicy movie on TV. I couldn't wait to get back to the solidity of my own space.

The place was too dark. There were no cars in the parking lot, no security lights brightening up the outside. There appeared to be lights on in a couple of the rooms. But it was awfully quiet for that time of night. I dashed into the room, locked the door and thought about taking a long soaky bubble bath, my favorite self-indulgence. Unexpectedly, the idea made me uneasy. I went right to my nightshirt, micro-waved popcorn, and snuggled down on the queen sized bed while I chose a movie. For some reason, I kept all of the lights on in the room. I couldn't get comfortable; I kept getting up, refreshing my diet drink, telling myself that I was in paradise. Without warning the voice inside said:

Get up. Get dressed. Get out. Now.
Get up. Get dressed. Get out. Now.

The hair on my arms stood at attention. I tried talking myself out of believing what I was hearing. I was just spooking myself. The place was a little old fashioned, but nothing like the Bates motel. I could go to sleep and everything would alright in the morning.

Get up. Get dressed. Get out. Now. The message was relentless. I remembered the other times the voice had told me to leave the Outer Banks before a hurricane came, or to get off the road and check my tires. Could I afford to test it now? Absolutely not. I jumped off the bed, pulled on my jeans under the shirt, stuffed everything into a bag and ran out the door to the van. My hand was shaking so badly I couldn't get the key in the lock right away. The clock on the dashboard informed me it was only 10:30 PM. Maybe I should go to the office and tell them I was leaving. Then I saw a curtain twitch as though someone were watching me from a darkened room and that was it. Get out. Now.

A brand name economy motel in the center of town was the only other alternative unless I wanted to drive for an hour into Albuquerque. The parking lot was mostly full, lights surrounded the building and the office manager was clearly visible through the window. I grabbed the same bag I had dumped on the floor of the van and walked into the welcoming lobby. The woman behind the desk looked up, smiled as though she knew me, and said, "Good evening. We have a nice room for you here. Nice and secure." I didn't bother to question how she knew.

And so it was I ended that day in a sterile, clean but safe room covered with blankets, a phone next to the bed, and sanitary, serviceable carpet on the floor. I slept the sleep of the innocent until the next morning when I headed up the highway to Albuquerque and the foot of the Sandia mountains, leaving the past and fear behind. I hoped.

By mid-day I was hooked-up to electricity and water, had walked the perimeter of a lonesome sandy campsite, and had explored the Common Room where there was a television, a small library, and comfortable chairs for reading when seeking shelter from the mountain winds. In one of those moments of synchronicity, which I was learning not to question, I heard from my weekly call to my son that longtime friends from home were enroute to Albuquerque and hoped we could connect *if I were anywhere near the area.* Dave passed on the message with the phone number of a couple who had retired to Albuquerque, and whom I knew slightly.

"Jean! We're so happy to hear from you!" Judy bubbled over the phone. "Where are you?" When I told her the direction of the campsite, she immediately jumped in with,

"Way out there? You don't want to be on the west side. Listen, we have plans for tonight, but tomorrow we'll come get you and you can have dinner with us, how would that be?" Actually, that would be really fine because the campsite was expensive, desolate and I had eaten Judy's food on numerous occasions when they lived in Massachusetts. It rivaled any cuisine anywhere. It certainly had greater appeal than microwaving in the van.

Meanwhile, I was free to explore Old Town: sopapillos (little pillows of deep- fried dough that you can fill with honey) at La Placita, a restaurant with an old tree growing in the middle of it. I could find the Indian museum and get literature on what exploring I wanted to do. There was a new Petroglyph Park where the carvings in the rocks were exposed for tourists to walk around and view.

"Yes," I thought, "I can be happy here for a long time. I can write in the mornings and explore in the afternoons." And, of course, there was always Santa Fe and Taos farther up in the mountains where the myths of Beauty and Spirit were said to dwell.

The friends of friends were true to their word. They took me to their comfortable suburban home and fed me the most delicious Iranian food I had ever eaten. Actually, it was the only Iranian food I had ever eaten. They had both been raised out of the United States as children of missionaries. He had been reared in Tehran and she in the Caribbean. Most of their married life had also been spent out of the country as his work took them all over the world: Iran, Egypt, Libya, and Somalia. Places they were eager to talk about. Places they articulated so completely they inspired visions and longings to see for myself. What a thought! There might be other trips after this one?

Well-read, well-educated, well-traveled, with working knowledge of several languages the couple had varied interests ranging from politics to religion to music to movies to fine food and wines. It wasn't hard at all to be a guest in their home! When the evening was over, I stayed the night, which stretched into two to save them from having to drive me back to the campsite. It was no sacrifice.

"Please come back in two weeks and stay with us when the our mutual friends are in town," Judy invited. "You won't want to drive back and forth to that awful campground when they're here. We'll have one big house party!"

In my head I weighed the wild but beautiful, lonely *and expensive* campsite versus the fascinating *free* hospitality of cosmopolitan generosity. Agreeing to return, I decided to use the two week hiatus as a golden chance to head north toward Santa Fe. What I did not know at that juncture was how this one acceptance would be the shift that profoundly changed the rest of my journey.

From that point on, with only a couple of notable exceptions, I would no longer be the lone lady camping and writing her way around the country. I would be joining with others once again, learning to live from the inside out while being distracted and bombarded by the demands and schedules of friends and family.

At that point I became in many ways a typical vacationing tourist. My work schedule was sent flying while my intentions, listening times and writing had to be fitted in and around someone else's life. The times that I could carve out for myself over the last three months of my journey would become even more precious, more productive and more deeply satisfying. But I was not to know any of that when I dived head-first into the house party invitation.

II
Santa Fe and...

Poor Falcon! It had altitude sickness trying to maintain speed on the wonderfully long passes leading ever up to Santa Fe and an elevation of 7200 feet. Having our fill of cities for the time being, the Falcon and I continued on into the outback to Lake Cochiti where the Army Corps of Engineers maintained a campground overlooking a dam and a lake.

It was a rarified spot high up in the mountains with views of rugged red rock formations. There was such a Mars-scape feeling to those pinion covered hills and mountains. Masked Dancers assuredly lurked behind every bush waiting to cry out their ancient tribal chants. Mystery fairly danced with the wind over the sparse high desert plains as far as I could see.

Excited about finding such a spiritual place where I could isolate at will, I was also close enough to Santa Fe to see its sights before I headed back down the mountain to reconnect with friends. This would be a place where I could accomplish so much from the inside-out. It was exactly what my soul yearned for after the cumulative experiences of getting here from Tucson. I held my God's Eye in front of my face and yelled, "I can feel it!"

I felt it all the way to the bathroom where I discovered the first and the most devastating drawback to my idyllic aerie. There were no showers! The bathhouse was a toilet and sink house only. And the Falcon had been denuded of its shower capabilities to make way for my clothes. All of which I would have gladly traded for one hot shower two days later. Adding to this was the unfortunate spring wind that came up every afternoon prohibiting being outside.

I wrote in my journal: "When that dry southwest wind blows, it dries the mouth, the nose, and the mind. Grit and sand have dug into my hair and permeated every bite of food. It does force me to stay in the van and write, however, a living metaphor for inside-out." Ms. Pollyanna stuck it out for four days of spitz baths before she cried, "Hold…enough," and trekked down off the mountain into Santa Fe to the Los Campos RV Park where she immediately fed two dollars in quarters into the slot for a long hot shower.

Prayers become so basic when life is reduced. I was thankful for hot water, conditioner and moisturizer. I lasted four days in the wilderness. How did anyone do it for forty? What about all the people who have no choice but to live under debilitating conditions, carrying water for miles, using water that is contaminated, or having no access to shelter from the dry desert winds? I apologized to God and all my unknown sisters and brothers around the globe for my childish complaints and the remarkable pettiness of my needs.

I called another friend, a psychiatric nurse practitioner, whom I had known and admired from hospice days. She had taken a job in a hospital in Santa Fe so it seemed like a good idea to call her. Joanne was insistent that I leave Los Campos and stay at her place for the week.

"Come do my life with me," is the way she put it. I wasn't quite sure what that meant, so put it down to Santa Fe-speak. "There are good people here for you to meet. You'll love the conversations. Believe me, you can o.d. on spirituality," she joked.

"You have to work every day," I reminded her.

"Look, you can have the run of the apartment. Cook. Meditate. Whatever it is you're doing. My son might be in and out, but he's not into talking to parental figures just now. If you ignore him, he'll ignore you." I wasn't sure about that.

"Can I set up my computer somewhere so I don't have to keep unplugging while I'm working?" I began to equivocate.

"Of course! And look on the bright side. You don't have to go to the laundromat." That last shot hit me true. The laundromat had grown old, despite the people I met there. It had become the pebble in my shoe.

So once again I acquiesced to someone else's itinerary and moved into her house, irrationally miffed at everyone's assumption that they were rescuing me from the awful fate of living in the Falcon.

I quickly lost my pique in the immersion of art galleries and handmade Native American jewelry on the boardwalk, all displayed with magnificent mountain views as backdrop. Santa Fe's opulence in the midst of small town southwestern charm overwhelmed the senses. I feasted on roaming, looking, and browsing. Four miles a day I hiked around the town, up and down hills and through the shops whose goods were way beyond my dwindling resources. When Joanne got home we walked some more, talked non-stop about life and purpose, being single and mothering, and God and all the holy angels.

'We met friends for supper downtown and had our tarot cards read *right there in the restaurant.* I was surprisingly nervous about what I might hear, but didn't want to appear wussy in front of Joanne and her friends.

"You are on a long journey." the grandmotherly woman told me. "You are finding your balance," she went on pumping me right up. "You are a woman of wisdom doing your great work." Better and better.

"Can you tell me some more about what my great work is?" I asked.

"You know what your work is," she dismissed my concerns with a smile. Then she added something else.

"You are becoming a wise Old Crone."

I had read extensively about the concept of the feminine and the onset of age that brings with it wisdom and the ability to *hold* the journeys of others, to help them on their way, to be a passer-on of truth. It was not that I had anything against the concept of women being Crones. I just didn't feel ready yet. Surely I wasn't old enough.

"Can't I be a Queen for just a little longer?" I half-jokingly asked her.

She patted my hand. "Get used to it, Sweetie." she laughed. Then she looked at me straight on and clear adding, "It is an honor to be a Crone. We all have our God-given gifts, don't waste yours." What started out as a lark ended on a spiritual note with the confusing ring of truth.

Later we went to the outdoor craft market where I bought a pair of carved silver earrings in the shape of a dangling moon and star, the eternal symbols of the feminine. If I were to be a Crone, I would wear it proudly.

III
...Back Again

When the two weeks were up, I drove out of the mountains without regret, except for the paltry amount of writing I had managed. Nevertheless, a couple of ideas coalesced into new dictums. *I need a deep abiding spiritual connectedness not only to the divine but to other people of like minds and hearts.* Perhaps this is self-evident for most people, but after the week of far-ranging conversation and listening, I was coming to terms with the concept in a new way. It felt like a guiding principle. The week forcefully presented the reality that I feel most complete, serene, purposeful and happy when engaged with others in the pursuit of spiritual understanding. *Living from the inside out only works when I can actively engage in Life.*

The other was more mundane, yet more consciousness shaking. Listening all week to the shop talk of other therapists discussing their cases, as academically fascinating as they were, forced me to admit that I tuned out so frequently not because I didn't know the people they were talking about, but because I felt distanced from the material. *Clinical psychotherapy no longer had the power to move me intensely in my inner self.* That realization shook me deeply.

There I was, in the mountains of the southwest, far from home base and everything that had anchored me for so many years. Not an auspicious time to question my vocation, my job, my source of identity and income that I was going home to. Who would I be if I lost interest in being a therapist? Faithfully recording it all in my journal, I firmly closed the book on this new restlessness of the soul until another time. That was a topic I would gladly put off crying about until tomorrow. Or until I had time to spend in deep quiet and listening. Meanwhile, I was due back in Albuquerque.

May rapidly slipped away toward June while I had been playing. My promise to be in California was rapidly approaching and I did not yet feel ready to have my journey end. I missed that feeling of deep inner peace, that profound connection to the God Within that had become so much a part of living close to sea and sky and mountains and desert. I had writing yet to do! I needed to slow down, return to living close to the elements in some way.

My friends from back east arrived and I was ecstatic to see them, to have a touch of home. We had been friends since our fourth grade daughters introduced us. How could I not leave my intentional life to spend time with them? They were pleased that I had been invited to stay with them and make a house party. They took my acceptance as a forgone conclusion.

No one pretended to understand why I would prefer to go off on my own than stay where the amenities were so gracious. And in truth, there was a part of me that wondered also. Then I understood. To my friends, what I was doing was a lark, a time out of mind, not to be confused with living reality. Naturally they would see their invitations to become part of a household as an offering of salvation, saving me from the needless sterility and hardship of living in a camper. After all, who, given the choice of living in a camper or in a lovely suburban townhouse overlooking the Sandia Mountains would choose the first?

The last week of May was, like most of my life, lived on several levels. My friends honestly made me feel that I had been missed, which was a rare and touching tribute. Honesty compelled me to admit to myself that outside of family, I wasn't missing anybody. My biggest sense of urgency came not from being cut-off from *home,* but in being afraid that I wouldn't accomplish all that I needed to before the year ended. Time was moving too fast. Yet, paradoxically I shelved all that and rationalized one more week to be on vacation.

The men played golf while we women spent hours in Old Town soaking up the art and culture. We cooked up a storm in Judy's kitchen, gabbing relentlessly while she stormed through the room leaving cupboard doors hanging open. I trailed behind her compulsively closing them just as quickly after replacing bags of spices and utensils. Her energy was boundless and her willingness to share her secrets a gift.

At dinner she dramatically dressed us in the intricately embroidered gabiyas of Middle Eastern women, posing us for pictures while we ate and drank and talked of politics and argued the place of religion in our lives. They were intellectually skeptical of anyone or anything directing my inner voice and thoughts. It was one against four.

"Oh come on, Jeanie. You don't really believe that God talks to you, do you?" My stomach did its familiar dive when challenged to defend the mystical, the sacred and the holy. I knew I was on shaky ground with these brilliant rationalists who tended to reason in linear terms. I was also aware of how sincerely each of them was dedicated to improving the lives of everyone, including the marginalized and the outcasts of all cultures. These were truly good people.

I took the plunge and told them how I had been living and traveling by waiting for the inner voice to guide me. "And just recently I heard that voice loud and clear in a motel room." When I finished my story there was a silence not altogether comfortable.

"And you think this voice was God?" challenged my friend. "Couldn't it have just been your own intuition, your own sense of self-preservation? God knows we've all had that." Both men had been teenagers when drafted into WWII. "There are plenty of stories out of every dangerous situation when people's adrenaline was on overload, a heightened awareness or alert to danger. They don't call it God! It's called biology."

My ire and frustration rose exponentially. I wasn't speaking theoretically; I knew there was something else and felt totally frustrated at my inability to articulate it. "I just know what I heard and what I experienced," I finished lamely. "That voice was as real and as separate from me as you are!"

"Then why doesn't God talk to all of us and save us a lot of grief?" the argument went on. "Why are you the only one who hears it and gets out of the way of trouble? What about the Iraqis and the Kuwaitis and all those people starving in Ethiopia and Somalia?"

I mutinously snapped back, "I don't know! And besides, who says I'm the only one? Look at all the books, the scriptures, the stories of the mystics who have been talking and writing about this for millennia!" I yelled out. "In every culture!" I added for good measure for the cosmopolitan among us and to be true to my ecumenical spirit.

"So, God sits on the throne waiting for us to petition for good things to happen. And some of us get through and others don't," the logic continued.

"No! I didn't say God is out there somewhere separate from us waiting to be asked. I think," I say with some hesitancy, "that God is in here," pointing to my chest, "within each of us. So maybe what I'm saying is that the Voice of the Divine, the Creator, whatever name you give, comes to us through the filter of our own selves. Our own nature," I tacked on trying to think it through while I talked, in true extrovert fashion.

The women broke in with stories of their own about how they knew things that went beyond reason. "I wouldn't say it was God. But I do think there is intuition which you could call a spiritual quality to life," Judy adjudicated.

"It's the highest of the Self," Joan agrees. "There is something in humanity that inspires us to be better than we are. I agree with Judy. I would call that spiritual."

"Yes," I agreed relieved for the reprieve. "Maybe we're just arguing over semantics. Maybe the name or what we call it isn't as important as being open to the fact that there is something *other* that we don't know what to name. In ancient Jewish scripture God said, 'No one knows my name.'" Ignoring the snorting of the men, I smiled at the women. Another disaster averted. Although, I knew in that same inner space that it wasn't about semantics. But I hadn't the words to make a difference and it saddened me.

One thing was certain, conversation never lagged with that group. I was left, however, with the nagging thought that I was not very expert in explaining the inexplicable because I could not fall back on absolutes as they seemed to be able to do. Where was the Crone when I needed her? Another entry for my journal of things to contemplate when I got back on the road and had time and peace.

I talked everyone into climbing the escarpments at the Petroglyph Park to see the carvings and became aware that my friends were several years older than I. As energetic and willing as they were, I was forced to face the truth that bodies change as we age to the late sixties, are not as agile, and that I, too, was heading inexorably in that direction.

I stood in the sunshine of that warm May day staring up at the face of the rocks watching my friends carefully find their footsteps and knew that I was looking at my own future. I prayed that I would have the same resiliency and humor about the coming of aging, that my mind was as sharp as my older friends. Even so, I was touched by a melancholy stemming from the same place of observation and distance I had felt in Santa Fe. I wasn't really a part of this group either. Was it age, circumstance, outlook, or guiding principles that separated us?

It was a good week, but I was truly ready to move-on after living the spring in other people's homes and territories. The time had been one of coming to grips with what I had labeled *distracters and enhancers* in the early part of my trip. Perhaps I was learning how to get back into the *ebb and flow* of life's realities. However, I was still seeking, still journeying and anticipating the culmination of the trip. I still wanted to explore the possibilities of self, others, the world and *God*—whatever that meant. Even so, there were hugs and kisses and well wishes as they waved me out of the driveway. "Be careful!" they all said in one way or another. "Be sure to let someone know where you are."

Inwardly I sighed. I only wished I knew where I was.

Book V

Summer:

*West Coast and
Back Home*

Chapter 19
Down to the Sea Again

Sea Fever

*I must down to the seas again, for the call of
the running tide
Is a wild call and a clear call that may not be
denied.*

*I must down to the to the seas again, to the vagrant
gypsy life,
To the gull's way and the whale's way where the wind's like
a whetted knife;
And all I ask is a merry yarn from a laughing
fellow rover,
And quiet sleep and a sweet dream when the
long [trip's] over.*
John Masefield

Looking at a map and knowing I could go anywhere I chose shivered my body and touched my soul with freedom, blowing out any malingering cobwebs left over from being housebound. Should I head toward Southern California or meander farther north toward the Grand Canyon? I had two and a half weeks before meeting my brother in Half Moon Bay on the coast side just south of San Francisco. Where could

I go to wallow in Falcon ease? I practically panted with the need to sleep on my own sturdy little pull-out bed, to lean over and turn on my coffeepot at dawn. Lounging against pillows with a hot cup in my hand watching the sun lazily curve itself through the slats of my blinds would be pure bliss. The quiet joy of being responsible for myself wrapped me in contentment.

I was in trouble. Craving that deep inner peace had become an addiction. I definitely got noodgy when I was away from the practice of deep centering for too long. What did that augur for a normal life when I returned home?

With such thoughts humming through my mind-chatter, I didn't leave Albuquerque until after one more of Judy's gifted noon tables. The infernal high desert afternoon winds were severe enough that by the time I reached Gallup I had had enough fighting both the van and the latent fears still ghosting around after west Texas. Once that door opened, my mind-numbing fears came trotting out. The worst, of course, was my continuing anxiety over having a flat tire in the middle of a hot desolated desert.

Oh the vagaries of what haunts our self confidence! Anything mechanical challenges my common sense and freezes my competence, making me feel inept and out of control. The map showed me that no matter which direction I chose, I had miles of desert to cross before I could smell the salt sea air.

I ticked off the miles across the cooler elevations of northern Arizona. Holbrook, Flagstaff, Kingman, all familiar places in my younger life, but no longer having power to lure me into the past. Then the road dropped down into the windy hot desert of Needles, California, through the Sacramento Mountains and across the Mojave Desert. Hot, humid, monochromatic, the landscape was painted with a terrifying starkness that intensified my primitive fears of survival in a place of unrelieved isolation. I kept driving into forever, a frightful reenactment of West Texas, until I landed at a gas station in Barstow where the wind almost ripped off the door.

More than ever, I knew I must get down to the sea again, down to the tides and the freshening smells. Down to great waters I couldn't see across. Down where the notes of the water gods playing their music night and day boomed across the wet sand. Down to where the water created lushness and temperate climes. I groaned in recognition of how desperate I was for the moist fecund juiciness of living water.

As if in response to my continuous beseeching, the next day was comfortingly calm, as was I. Up over the mountains and down into the San Bernardino Valley to Ventura and the coast appeared the most judicious course. Gradually, the terrain began to change shape. Rounded and moss green the elevated vistas were unlike anything I had seen so far. The mountains were soft, almost touchable, with occasional jagged cuts for the road through them imparting the sense that I was floating down into a golden valley.

In one quick jolt my idyllic vistas morphed into a huge urban megapolis. Los Angeles? It couldn't be! Where was Ventura? What had I done? I moaned as the city crept inexorably closer.

"No, no!" I panicked. "I can't do this!" Terrified that I would be swept up in L.A. freeway traffic and lost forever, I frantically took the next exit. The travel angel was once again on my shoulder. It only took one fairly uncomplicated backtrack and my blood pressure returned to normal as I once again wended my way toward the coast and Ventura. More than ever quiet coastal waters and a leisurely meander northward were necessary to my survival.

Then suddenly, up over another rise and there spread below were valleys filled with orchards! Bountiful and beautiful there were cherry trees, oranges, lemons, as far as I could see. The air was cool and sweet. Fruit stands everywhere were selling fresh strawberries and other seasonal agriculture. Paradise of a thousand dreams spread out before me. I had fallen asleep and landed in a paradise of food and water and lush green growth. Lunch was a basket of cherries, a bag of strawberries and a bite of cheese. I wanted to run through the fields, lie down with the leaves and smell the fresh goodness of the earth. But this wasn't camping land and I still had miles to go to find the sea.

Like the East Coast, the West Coast has its old original road that follows along the water. I was so entranced with the views and the ride I barely recall Ventura as I flew up Route 1 north to Santa Barbara, ecstatically gulping cool water views. I had forever wanted to see that coastal hillside town, home to writers I admired and the background of novels and movies. In some tiny part of me I harbored a secret thought that I might move there. But that was not the year.

I walked to the edge of the downtown park drinking in the ocean air and enjoying the palm trees so precisely planted. Listening to the cacophony of a major resort town, I heard my inner voice insist that I must climb back in the Falcon and carry on. This was not the place. This was not the time to move into someone's apartment or do her life or play tourist. If I wasn't certain what the time was for, it didn't matter. There would be a quieter spot just up the coast. I knew it.

Certainty did not prevent the deflated feelings of disappointment and loneliness sweeping through me, however. Was it possible that I was becoming tired of living on the edge of not knowing what was coming next? Again, I slammed the door on thoughts I wasn't prepared to deal with at the moment.

It occurred to me that I had been slamming the door a lot lately. There were a goodly number of issues packed away in that holding room somewhere in the basement of my self-awareness. Mentally compiling a list while I drove north, I concentrated on trusting that the Divine truly had a place in mind for me to stop and rest and plug-in. The list later showed up in my journal:

- *questioning my vocation as a therapist*
- *changing the nature of my relationships when I returned home*
- *questioning my purpose and accomplishments on the journey*
- *looking at the absolutes in my life, what I "know" and my inability to articulate them*

And finally, that most recent thought:

- *that I was preparing to re-enter mainstream living again and I was questioning how and where*

El Capitan Beach. Campsites were right on the water with miles of trails for walking and biking. Long climbing stairways fell over the cliffs to the limitless vistas of Pacific beaches. I pulled in and was disappointed to discover that there were no electrical hookups. The helpful park ranger pointed out a private campground across the road which did not have the advantage of water views, but did have hot showers and electricity for my computer. All the amenities of the state park were just across the road. So it was that I settled in once again, content in the beauty of the space and thrilled to be snuggled in with my Falcon.

Trucks, vans, station wagons and cars pulled in letting loose a tumultuous band of folks who loudly set up tents, a huge canvas screen room, and unloaded enough coolers and food to feed the whole campground.

"Great," I moaned. "Just great. All I want is a little peace in which to talk to God and a family reunion invades!" I sat in my chair under my awning shooting evil thoughts and words at the interlopers who dared to interfere between me and the spiritual life. "They'll be drinking beer to all hours. Screaming kids will be running everywhere. Double damn," I kept up the grousing. "When will I ever get the peace and quiet I crave?" I slammed into my van and pulled down the shades for the night determined to shut out the din from the uncivil neighbors.

By the time I had talked myself into leaving in the morning, made up the bed in a huff, and was trying to read a junk novel, I heard the first riff of a guitar. There was no noisy bombast from the family reunion across the way; there was simply the rise of soulful voices singing together in harmony. Singing songs of peace and joy; singing songs I had known since childhood of faith, and trust. Giggling children's voices were singing silly songs requiring motions. Standing up and sitting down, putting your right and left hands in, co-mingled with the quieting songs of day's end. Until at last, they ended with *Just a Closer Walk with Thee.*

I lay there in the dark listening with my whole soul, singing along, letting the tears come as a cleansing gift to once again wash away my rush to judgment, my negativity, and my preconceived ideas. "Oh, God," I moaned. "How often have I cut off experiences of you and missed opportunities to know others because of my arrogance?"

Last weekend I was feeling inarticulate and alienated in the midst of friends; this weekend I was feeling in harmony with strangers. There was a message there, but it was one more thing that I would have to think about tomorrow. I never knew I had such Scarlett tendencies.

With daylight I learned that I had the family reunion half right. It was a Family Retreat from St. Paul's Episcopal Church. Not only had they closed their evening circle with my grandmother's favorite hymn, the next morning I found out they were from a church with the same name as the one I currently belonged to back home. Their retreat leader was known for his compositions as well as his retreats designed around interactive music. He sent the teenagers out to tag all the campsites with invitations to join with the families the following day for their Sunday morning session and Eucharist.

I had not shared a liturgy of communion for many months. The invitation to take part once again in the sacramental breaking of bread and drinking of wine recalled me to my roots with a hunger I hadn't known was there.

When I walked across the common the next morning to join with the families of St. Paul's, a thousand images danced in my head of all the spiritual retreats I had been part of in the last thirty years in many guises from participant, to designer-facilitator. In truth, one of the sacrifices made for this year of living from the inside out was canceling requests to present, facilitate or lead Spiritual Retreats. How ironic. I stopped my life and left home in order to listen, and end up listening to how someone else does what I did at home. I hurried forward, eager to join in and experience the Spirit at work, aware that interests dormant for almost a year were stirring to life. Who knew what professional tips I might pick up?

The families made room in their screen room for a stranger. I arrived in time to be assigned to one of the several small groups meeting that morning to design and prepare the worship service. Naturally, in God's humorous way of giving me *practice,* my group was in charge of coming up with a worshipful way to bring meaningful closure to the weekend using interactive music. In other words, I got to say *goodbye* one more time.

Again I was rocked back on my past. A Sufi song I learned at a retreat in Alaska twenty years before was the one we settled on for the final benediction of the morning. A simple, powerful song that we sang in a prayerful stance as each singer looked directly into the eyes of one other person. At the last line both singers touched their palms together then moved on to the next person, repeating the song until all have danced and sung into the eyes, hands and heart of every other person present.

Listen, listen, listen
to my heart's song.
Listen, listen, listen
to my heart's song.
I will never forget you;
I will never forsake you.
I will never forget you;
I will never forsake you. (Repeat)

There was no hiding of the self when you sang this while looking into the laughing eyes of children, the somewhat chagrined, sometimes cynical eyes of adults and the shy eyes of adolescents, or the knowing eyes crinkled with years of living of the elders. These are the words of God's promise whispered directly to all people. These are the words that each of us needs to promise in order to be connected to others in a profoundly spiritual and deeply human way. They are the words of God passing through each of us into the other. *I will never forget you; I will never forsake you...*

I was making promises to people I had never met nor seen before that moment, yet I was transported by the music into the realm of mystical positive knowing that transcends reason and logic. Our reason for *being* is our commitment to the Divine and to all of humanity and creation, as is God's to us. For a few moments in the ongoing story of my life, I promised neither to forget nor to forsake what I learned from each one of the persons I sang to, and who sang to me. The lingering melody of that California seaside morning among strangers would be for then and for always to *listen, listen, listen* to the heart's song of each and every person I dance with in this lifetime.

Within a short time after the last note of the song, the families

205

retreated to their weekday lives leaving behind an empty campground but one full camper, grateful for a renewed sense of belonging. Of course, I bought the retreat leader's song book to add to my collection. Perhaps there would be an opportunity down the pike for me to engage in a longer intentional retreat.

How strange, I thought, *the ocean is on the wrong side of the road.* How disorienting to be traveling north and to have the water on my left. On the east coast, it would be on my right. I was honestly all turned around.

It was time to map out my primary objectives for the next couple of weeks. The urgency sprang from the growing reality that once I met my brother, my trip as I had designed it was over. I would not have the luxury of taking months to wend my way back to the east coast. Down to the wire, I should make creative use of the solitude left to me. It was back to basics; back to intentions, daily disciplined schedule, to writing and to making my own music.

Pismo Beach was authentic beach camping. Huge dunes blocked the sturdy wind rushing from the water where the beaches again stretched out forever. The first of the west coast fog rolled in, reminding me that I was heading north toward San Francisco Bay where summer is more like a chilly, damp fall. I hated to complain, after all the moaning I had done a few days ago about desert heat and lack of humidity. I had forgotten the bone chilling dampness of fog and ocean breezes. Hunkering down behind mountainous sand dunes seemed like a protected place to pull in and write. The park ranger promised that the sun burned off the fog, usually, by early afternoon. Perfect. Half the day to stay indoors and write, and half the day to walk, exercise and explore the beach. Same old, same old.

My enthusiasm was tempered with the familiar itchy restlessness I had not experienced since the cold night in January when I finally admitted that I wanted something more from my life than I was currently living. Contemplating what those new vague stirrings might be, I stared at the picnic table before me, unfocused and deep in thought. Something in my periphery brought me back into the present.

A huge crumb was on the move.

Way down at one end of the table a little brown ant slowly struggled forward, heading down the table to the opposite end. On his back was an impossibly heavy crumb three times his size. A leftover from my picnic lunch, I supposed. Slowly, slowly, one agonizing inch at a time, he came toward me, focused and single-minded. I looked at the table and thought, *You're never going to make it. This table is huge for you! You'll fall through a crack.*

Mesmerized, I didn't move. "It's going to take you all day to get down there," I told him." I could not turn away as he struggled on. I knew he was taking the crumb back to *The Hill* where it would help feed his cohorts. I remembered that from Bio 101. Never daunted, he moved around a nail head sticking up in his path, slowing him only slightly. "Don't you just want to rest a bit and have a chew?" I asked him, leaning down to eye level. "Take your time? Savor the moment? Who would know?" He ignored my tempting and persevered.

"Look at you!" I marveled. "This table is as long as...as...the whole state of California would be for me. You probably can't even see where it ends but you just keep on carrying your load, instinctively heading back to base."

Aha. I felt the click somewhere in my heart region. That little ant was doing nothing more or less than what he was put here to do. He was carrying his bundle, as Thomas Kelly had written, doing what he could to shore up and feed his community. And in that moment, I envied him with all the yearning inside me. He knew what his bundle was and where he belonged. While I, I sat there three thousand miles from home knowing that within a short time I would be heading down my own long table. I could not see the end, but I knew that defining my bundle, feeding the community and heading instinctively for my base were just as authentic for me as for my very *big* guru ant.

"Hey, Jean," my brother called down the wire, "where are you? Getting close to Half Moon Bay?"

"Sure am. I headed up through Big Sur today and I'm still a little stunned."

"Incredible, isn't it? How did the van do on the curves?"

"Nobody warned me, Dave, how narrow the road really is. I can't tell you how many times I pulled into a scenic overlook to let the traffic behind me go ahead. It was mortifying!" My brother guffawed.

"At least you were on the right side of the road." he chuckled. "Going south you would have been on the outside with nothing between you and the cliffs to the ocean."

"Believe me, I was grateful the whole way. There were still hairy moments when I met monster RV's and buses coming the other way that expected me to hug the inside. Mostly, though, I was in a state of blissful awe at the majesty of the scenery. I'm camped tonight right on the Big Sur River in a stand of trees where I can hear the sound of the water playing over the rocks. Back in there it could be Vermont or New Hampshire.

"No it couldn't..."

"Save it, Mr. Biology. I know the trees are different, but the atmosphere isn't." I interrupted him before he could lecture me on flora and fauna. "I'm really just checking in to see how much longer I have on the road by myself. I plan to hit your house the day you have finished checking, grading, and handing in reports and not a minute before."

"Good, 'cause I'd be lousy company anyway. Why don't you get here next Wednesday? The door's open. And Jean?"

"Yes?"

"I have some great plans for us. It's been a good year. Kids have been great, but I need to get away."

"Like what kind of plans?" I asked, expecting the guy who used to live on his sail boat to talk of getting out on the Bay and shore dinners on the dock at Sausalito. I wouldn't turn down crab at the Embarcadero or something decadent at Ghiardelli Square, either.

"I'm always so exhausted when the year finally winds down that I usually just take my sleeping bag into the redwoods. I really want to get up into Gold Rush country or Lake Tahoe area. Maybe both, depending on time. You know, do a little camping, a little roughing it. If you stick around long enough, I can show you Yosemite."

I bit back the groan. Camping? Roughing it? He was so hopefully childlike I didn't have the will to bring my hidden agenda into the sunshine.

"By the way," he went on. "Two of your favorite Germans will be here for July 4th. So you have to stick around till then. They already put in their request for sailing out to the island in the Bay for a picnic and dinner in Sausalito."

I hung up with bittersweet feelings swirling through my psyche once again. Eager as I was to see the young people who had been so much a part of our family since the exchange programs of high school, I wanted to grow beyond all these tugs back into the consciousness of *then*. If I stayed until July to see these young adults whom I had grown to love over the years, I would definitely be making the choice to circumscribe the rest of my journey. Were they *distracters or enhancers?*

As I walked back to my campsite I let go of these ruminations. Life is what it is. Peace settled into my soul. I knew that it was okay. *Life is about relationships.* I was being given an opportunity to strengthen mine with my brother, and with a surrogate son and daughter. How could I not hear the *inner voice* in that, or see the hand of God gently opening? Definitely enhancers.

II
Back and Forth

Looking back on that time with my brother I still laugh at some of our antics. I forgot my glasses when I did the shopping and went way over budget when I paid twenty-five dollars for some meat that I honestly thought was twelve. He tried to roast a stuffed pork tenderloin in a makeshift stone oven because he forgot that we didn't have electricity for roasting.

We had not spent that kind of time together since childhood. One week stretched into two as we toured all the spots he mapped out. I had grudgingly given in to the more isolated campsites without hookups that he craved and was thankful every moment. The dense quiet of pristine wilderness hushed our internal strivings with wisps of nature's voices blanketing the sounds of civilization. There was such peace.

But what I remember most was the talking. We talked about the embarrassments of Big Sister-Little Brother incidents of childhood, exorcising old hurts and lending each other comfort in our personal losses. We marveled at our fortune in the rediscovery of the blessedness of a sibling from whom we did not have to hide anything. *"Mother always did love me best, you know,"* Dave loved to tease. Quoting the Smothers Brothers, he was only half joking. And I was finally free enough to give it up and laugh along. We mourned the fact that as adults we had always kept a continent between us.

We made music together. Dave played the guitar and sang bass, while I stirred the campfire and sang melody. I can still see his face shadowed by the blush of the fire and hear his thrillingly rich baritone rolling solo into the dark. *"Away out here they have a name for earth and wind and fire…"* We danced around our worries about our aging parents, made feeble jokes about their doing us a favor by living forever. Our laughter laid bare our own fears; exposed us to our own reluctance to admit to aging. And we talked about what it will feel like when our parents are no longer here to shield us from being the last of our generation. Who else but a brother or a sister can share our lives on this deep and rich continuum from birth, if we but allow it?

That time with my brother was then, and still remains, a precious gift of my journey. It was more than healing. It exposed both the joy of being with someone who understood why I am who I am today, and the complexities of reconciliation to the realities of growing into the next stage freely and with a whole heart. I left him with the knowledge that we could not have done this in our twenties, or even our thirties, when our lives were lived so separately, our values so different.

His last words as he waved me out of his drive slipped past all defenses and teased the possibilities. "Next summer I'm going to Switzerland to see Alison and my new son-in-law and granddaughter. Why don't you meet me there? We can rent a car. Slip into France for a few days. Spend some more time together. Think about it."

The year before, I would have waved and sarcastically yelled, "Yeah, yeah, yeah. Sure Bro," knowing that with my schedule and finances it was a smoke dream. That year, however, I felt the bubble inside rising as I headed north over the San Francisco Bay Bridge and the sparkling water beneath. I had asked for getting back to the sea again, for wrapping myself on the shores where sky and water and sand came together and I got far more than I ever dreamed. Next summer? Who knew? In my forties I would never have believed that I could have had a year like the one almost behind me. The woman who left her brother's driveway was not the same woman who started out last fall.

Chapter 20

Desert to Dessert

There were no adjectives left in my vocabulary to describe the soaring beauty of mountain passes, roads where white pearl heat grabbed at tires, or the coolness of desert evenings brushing over hot skin like the beat of a thousand butterfly wings. On scenic tourist overload, I had feasted at the table of spiritual and physical abundance and could hold no more. The Falcon was overhauled, all systems checked and tires inflated to the correct number. The interior was clean and organized; frig full, cupboards stocked, and everything stashed for a sleek ride. We were more than ready to head back to whatever awaited us at journey's end. It was time to push back and make room for the final indulgence.

From the beginning of the trip, there were three predetermined places where I committed myself to be. I had completed two of them:

- Christmas in South Carolina with my children the previous December
- meeting my brother in California in June

Now it was July with only one promise unfulfilled. I needed to find the Lake of the Ozarks and discover what it was that I was supposed to do, meet, or be in that place. I had absolutely no idea where it was, what it was, or my purpose for getting off the main roads to get there. One last holy mystery; one last sweet following of the Inner Voice into the unknown. It had been an exciting way to travel thus far; I could not abandon it now. Besides, my curiosity demanded satisfaction. Where was this place?

The first night in northern California I stopped early to research this mysterious Lake of the Ozarks. All I came up with was Lake of the Ozarks State Park near Osage Beach, Missouri. Naturally in the grand scheme of things, it was on the way to my final destination of the summer: meeting my daughter in August at my parents' home in Indianapolis. The mystery was why anyone would choose to hurry toward the stifling humidity of a Missouri August instead of lingering in the cool elevations of the mountainous West?

Route 80 would take me all the way from California through Utah, Nevada, Wyoming and Nebraska almost to Missouri where I could pick up Route 70 through St. Louis into Indiana. Straight and simple. One highway cut through parts of the country I had never seen. I was especially keen to drive through the Great Salt Flats, those hundred miles or so of mirage inducing, shimmering white salt desert on the outskirts of Salt Lake City. In a strange way, passing through the Great Salt Lake would be my last connection to the primordial sea until I came full-circle to the great Atlantic on the east coast.

The choice would also scratch one of my sneaky mother itches. The route meant a drive through Park City, Utah, the absolutely only place in the country where my oldest son could find work, and coincidentally ski, for the long year when his family was fragmenting. "At least one person in my family will know where I lived and worked," he jokingly attempted on the phone when I told him my plans. Maybe by being there I could connect to his hurts, understand the pull and safety of the place.

Who was I kidding? The truth was that I needed the ritual cleansing, letting my child go with blessings to command his own adult pains and pleasures. *Bittersweet,* I thought, *the fruits of aging. Knowledge and understanding are not always palatable foods. Now I carry the knowledge that I cannot shelter anyone, especially those I love, from the content of their own choices.*

I flashed back to Mrs. Sanford and her perpetually blending stock on the back of the stove. Hovering new maturity told me that the most I could do was stir my son's stockpot. The bits and pieces of his life's leftovers would be the flavors of his own unique soup. I was learning through him to give others the *gift* of their own pain.

Two days into the trip the ultimate terrifying disaster struck. The Falcon blew a rear tire on a stretch of barren highway of nonexistent shade. Every fantasy and fear I had entertained about tires and heat and lonely desert roads gushed through my body.

Slightly beyond Battle Mountain, Nevada on a flamingly hot day near the end of July, I pulled the van to the shoulder, this time, *shaking* from the inside-out. Overcome with helplessness I could do nothing but slump over the steering wheel wailing until the feisty little three year old hiding deep inside jumped out to pummel on the door of my self-consciousness.

Utterly paralyzed and helpless, I opened all the doors to let the hot breeze blow through while I slouched, sweaty and red, on the couch to reconnoiter. One more time I went through the list of times I had listened, trusted and acted. If it were true that we attract to ourselves those things we are most anxious to ignore, I could at least rejoice that I had not feared murder, rape and arson. Next to those, what was a flat tire? At that precise moment, a state policeman knocked on the side of the Falcon before he leaned in the door.

"Your tire has lost the rubber, but it's still somewhat inflated," he told me. "I'm going to stop traffic and get you turned around across the road where you can head to the last exit about six miles back. There's a tire place just off the ramp. Now if you take it real slow, put on your hazards, you might make it. If not, I want you to stay right there and wait for me to come back. There's an accident further down the road that I'm already late getting to. But I will, repeat, *I will* come back to check on you."

I stammered some reply. Whatever it was, he smiled a crooked grin and tapped the Falcon's door as he walked out to the middle of the highway to stop a few trucks. It was probably something about angels or some other inside-out expression.

The drive to the tire place was palpitatingly slow as I compulsively repeated, "You don't have to panic," when semis shot past me shaking the van. Believe it or not, no one could miss the exit in the distance. The letters of the town were painted on the side of the mesa adjacent. BM was proudly displayed for planes and high desert traffic. Laughter roiled in my scatological gut as I inched my way closer. There, as was promised, just a little further, was the tire store. I pulled into the lot, turned off the ignition and the whole backend of the Falcon gently deflated with a sigh. The damaged tire got us exactly to safety, but no farther.

There was a nasty smell of burnt rubber, and I swore I could see smoke near the rear tire. The tire man discovered that the rear fender was bent under and the exhaust extender had shoved up inside and broken off. The heated exhaust was hitting directly on the tire. "Hell, Lady, you're lucky you didn't burn down your RV and half the highway."

Clearly blasé about the effect of his words, he compounded the news. "Your hub cap is way too hot for a flat. Here, feel this." He placed my reluctant hand on the scorching hub. "You gotta check this baby all the time on the road. If it's hot, something's wrong with your brakes probably. In your case, the emergency brake is hung up. The cable's all rusted and old."

Then he looked at me, really looked at me and echoed the words of a hot Florida day, "Geez, Lady, you must have an angel riding with you in this thing. Any one of these problems could have had your as—uh, sorry, could have killed you flat."

I must have blanched, for he looked slightly sorry for his outspoken behavior. I guess he was trying to be sociable when he added, "If you were heading for the salt desert, you are so damn lucky you got this fixed now, 'cause there's not a chance in hell that you would have survived out there. There's no services to speak of for a hundred miles." Leaving me to imagine burning up one way or the other on the road to Salt Lake City. For once I agreed with Dad. My imagination could definitely get overactive.

Choking on my own inchoate feelings, I drove across the salty desert in a state of otherworldliness akin to seeing everything from behind a glass enclosure. Terror of what might have been warred with a manic need to scream and cry out my thank-yous to the unseen hand that rescued me that day. I drove through Salt Lake City registering its clean classic façade but too immobilized to trust myself out of the van. I simply kept driving until I climbed into the welcoming coolness of the mountains where I found a quiet motel on the edge of a town where nothing was demanded of me other than my credit card. Depleted in body, wrung out spiritually and empty at last of all feeling, I curled into the comforter with the barely fleeting thought that I, too, was given the chance to heal from some of my fears in the town of Park City, Utah.

II
Lake of the Ozarks

Several days later after cruising down out of the pure mountain air of the west and barreling along the expansive amber grain-growing plains along the Platte River, I began to tense up. Shoulders ached, arms were rigid, my whole body went into fight or flight mode as I hunched over the steering wheel. The Falcon and I had driven straight into the urban-suburban-industrial Midwest with all the fumes, narrower roads, and zillions of commuters pummeling to be first. Why on earth would I want to spend the last of my time-capital closed-in in a park with too many people competing for privacy in mosquito infested humidity? The interminably open highways of the past eight months were already fading into the memories of history. I had re-entered the familiarity of frenetic hustling.

Faintly appalled by the ease with which I gunned the van for a fast lane change, I began to rethink the undesirability of holing up in a state park, humidity or no. At the very least, I would have a quieter camping experience instead of fighting traffic and people for every bit of room. My spirits dragged with the admission that whatever Lake of the Ozarks State Park held, it signaled the last time to be alone. I sincerely prayed that it be worthy of being the dessert of my elegant feast.

Cutting down country roads was a relief, but the topography suffered by comparison to the soul scorching scenery I had mournfully left behind. One entertaining fantasy after the other helped pass the time of the desultory drive. The one that held the greatest appeal was that I would meet Sam again; that he had survived the Gulf War. I would take a walk to the water and find him fishing with his son and we would...

The state park, in truth, was a sparkling jewel. Lush, green, towering deciduous trees lent their shade on a hot, lazy-hazy, humid summer afternoon. When I stepped out of the van, singing cicadas conjured up similar days of childhood in Kentucky and Ohio. All that was missing was the slam of the screen door followed by mom's warning voice as I escaped outside to play.

I picked my spot at the end of a row that afforded almost complete privacy. A shaded road led down to a narrow lake with beach and picnic areas a quarter of a mile away. I remember thinking, *Okay, God, this is all lovely and it sure beats congested traffic. I hate to complain, but peaceful as it is, it's not one of your most spectacular projects. Why did I feel so compelled from the start to be here?* My chummy attitude was met with silence.

For one and a half days all attempts to communicate with the Inner Voice were met with silence. Frustrating as it was, I never felt I was abandoned, I felt that I was waiting. So I used the time to sleep and repair the angst that had hovered since Black Mountain. I walked, swam, and wrote until sometime on the second day the meaning sank in. I was here to live into that sacred silence where God speaks. The last ten days of my journey were to be a spiritual retreat, a time to renew my intention, to have the luxury of assessing and integrating this past year's rich journey of body and soul unfettered by the ordinary. This would be a hallelujah time to go back through my journals, cull out the lessons, and delight once more in reliving the people and their stories. The time had come to discover the themes of my journey.

Taking paper and marker, I designed a retreat. Each day would be a *discipline* of schedule, theme and activity, including downtime and free time for writing, household chores and shopping. How efficient! My goal was to leave there having drunk every drop and chewed every morsel of sustenance I could hold before I willingly drove back into the life I left almost a year ago.

I tried so hard, sitting with newsprint at the picnic table, to pick seven themes for the seven days remaining. Seven neat little topics that would lend themselves to a retreat designed to sum up a year of incredible diversity and depth of thought and experience. *Listen, trust, act, creativity, relationships, writing, interactions with the mystical, transformation, reconciliation;* the list already overwhelmed me and it wasn't even complete. I knew then that it would take years for all the layers and complexities of themes and lessons to emerge into consciousness. But I, with my handy little magic marker and newsprint, was determined to get it all down, decently and in order, that day. Until, that is, I recognized that it wasn't working.

I got lost in the morass of details on each page of my journals. I got distracted into the tangential places where I laughed again over the bossy guys directing this neophyte trying to park the Falcon, and misted over cuddling little Billy when he gave up his balloon to the universe. At that rate, I could use up all seven days reading and designing without ever spending a moment in *retreat.*

By evening I was out of sorts, and discouraged from ever figuring out the best way to accomplish what I instinctively knew was important. Lulled by the deepening roseate evening and the sounds of crickets, birds and squirrels putting their young to sleep, I let all my frustrations and strivings go on the gentle winds of evening. A self-directed retreat was probably an oxymoron anyway. Naturally, that was the moment when clarity and purpose settled in. *Listen, listen, listen to my heart song...*

The overarching theme of the whole experience from its inception to that moment at Lake of the Ozarks was one of *listening.* Listening to the inner voice, of going to that place of silence where my voice, intellect and ego quieted so that when God spoke, I could hear. Why should my retreat be any different from the intentional way I had chosen to live from the inside-out? The framework of the design might be mine, but the *Inner Voice* would be in charge of the content each day.

III

The Finishing Touch

So it was that the last seven days blended into a rhythm of building and holding memories. I arose each morning to walk in the barely coolest part of the day, preparing myself physically for the unfolding to come. I prepared my mind by reading my journals; I prepared my spirit by quiet centering prayer and opening to the inner direction.

Very little stirring took place at other campsites. The quiet was disturbed only by the bass thrumming of dozens of air conditioners. There were no morning yells or children running and screaming, no clanging of pots and pans nor smells of bacon and coffee. For the first time all year, the distraction of convivial campers was not an issue. I was nonplussed after the gregariousness of other campgrounds that my neighbors huddled inside their rigs, coming out only to go to the lake or to drive out for the day. I could not have chosen a better place for a lack of environmental stimulation.

Well, there was one mildly disconcerting mystery that I never figured out. Occasionally I observed people leaving their artificially cool RV's throughout the day to toss more logs onto perpetually burning campfires. The wood snapped in the smoldering heat and sparks flew heavenward adding strong smoke to the thick oppressive air.

Yet it was within this dichotomy of disconnect, of being cut-off from contact in a relatively sterile environment, that I was called to listen to the first stirrings of what I needed to hold fast from the past precious, precious year.

Connection rolled through my consciousness like the tides of last fall. The entire year had been about the enormous varieties of connection extant in every living thing, every encounter, every event. I felt again the thread that runs through all of creation, weaving us into patterns of inter-dependence and beauty, and yes, sometimes fear, pain and grief. The same pattern exalts in the inner self-knowledge that we are never cut off, never alone. In order to get to this place of profoundly peaceful acceptance of living from the inside-out, I had to connect myself to a journey through the year once again.

I reconnected to my past, my childhood and family members in order to firmly anchor myself in my own origins. How could I possibly grow older wisely if I were not intimate with my true self? If I were not willing to strip myself down to *essence,* beyond expectations and roles? So I gave up that day any pretensions and glossing over of the hurt little three year old with her complex memories of growing up as a minister's daughter, and allowed her to have a voice for a little while.

Then I moved on to the songs and stories of grandparents and all those who had come before, claimed them, owned them, gave thanks for them in their perfect imperfection. The hurts that accrued throughout a lifetime were sent up on the smoke of all the campfires. Their power to torment drifted into the ether, leaving behind a distillation of effervescent joy. I did not know at the time that with this simple act of spontaneous ritual I had taken a huge step toward the reconciliation and integration of broken places I still called holes in the soul.

I allowed the half-formed young woman who married young, and lived to question the choice, to dance out into the sunshine of her older wisdom and be grateful for the rich life that was her reward, despite that choice. Enumerating those rewards on a banner were daily reminders of thankfulness throughout the process:

- parents and family who articulated and lived their values
- the concomitant joys and pains of a long-term marriage
- the holy fears and privileges of raising children
- a landscape of meaningful people and friendships
- my evolving clarity of loyalty and commitment to promises, ideas, and healing
- the enriching compassion of grief and loss
- opportunities for a broader worldview
- a deepening capacity to love
- an authentic sense of the availability of the divine, the holy and the sacred

From the cosmic to the specific I danced along the path of my year's journey, re-experiencing oneness with the life-giving seas and challenging mountains. I laughed aloud with the watchful deer, and joined hands with ants and every sort of creature I encountered. I sent up prayers of thankfulness for all the teachers in campgrounds, homes, and singles groups. All the while I was also, like the young Apache girl at sunrise, paradoxically dancing into the heart of connecting to myself.

The year was also about the *discernment* of the differences between *roles* and *identity*. The woman who cried in her upper room over the emptiness of her soul and the loss of identity and belonging had gradually, throughout the year, been waving goodbye as she retreated into the mists of shadow. Far from losing my identity, I was in the process of claiming my identity *independent* of the roles I had lived so many years.

The coming of aging meant my *roles* changed, as they change for everybody; and to some extent the identity with which the world labeled me as well. If I were no longer Mrs., no longer identified with a man, then who was I in our culture? If my children had outgrown their need for protective mothering, then what kind of mother was I to be? If I left my practice to journey across the country, then who was I professionally? If the mirror gave back an unfamiliar image, lined and rounded, then who was I becoming?

In retreat, I gathered up the threads of the woman I practiced being over the past year and began to understand that living from the inside-out meant far more at the end of the trip than at the beginning. I knew that I would always have roles in this life, but I vowed that they would be lived out of *who* I am not *what* I am. And the Inner Voice echoed *Amen.*

Finally, I knew that the year had given me the gift of *freedom* to listen, trust, and act. The ramifications went far beyond anything I could have imagined standing on the curb the year before, anticipating freedom as a sabbatical that meant a break from work and getting out from under the burden of debt and responsibilities. At that time my vision was limited to the anticipatory excitement of not living under the control of schedules, calendar, and checkbook.

At the end of the journey I knew that my experiences of freedom took me into places of the soul where I was *free from* the fears that haunt and ultimately govern so much of life when we are defined by our external roles and expectations, our looks and the judgments of others. At the same time, the gift was also to be *free to* discover new ways of being and creating in the next stage of life. *Perhaps the greatest gift of the coming of aging is the freedom to accept the essence of self and others without pretensions or judgment, and begin the journey toward the place where we started: unconditional love.* Sitting under a tree at

Lake of the Ozarks, I remembered something my dad said to me years before.

When I was eighteen, he came to the college campus where I was a freshman and took me out to lunch. Over dessert I confessed the resentment I felt before I left home over the lack of freedom my parents exercised by imposing horribly unfair curfews.

"I would get so mad at you and mom for making me come home from a dance before everyone else," I somberly told him. "It was so unfair! If I was one minute late mom would campus me." Dad just listened, half smiling at this old ground. "Remember how I fought to get you guys to let me stay out until one o'clock? I couldn't wait to grow up and get away to school where I would be free!"

"And are you?" he asked. "Free, that is?"

"You wouldn't believe what they do at this school," I wailed. "Freshmen women have to be in the dorm by 9:30 on week nights and eleven on weekends until the first grades are posted. If you get a C+ average you can stay out a half-hour later. If you're not in by per time, you get expelled!" Dad merely shrugged and smiled. "I thought I was going to be so free here, and it's worse than it was at home!"

He leaned over the table and took my fisted hand in his looking me straight in the eye. "Haven't you learned yet, young lady, that you are only *free* in this life when you are *bound* to things that are worthwhile?"

There I was, thirty-five years later and just beginning to get a small harvest from the seed he planted that day. When I allow myself to live out of the essence of who I am, then what I do comes from the holiest of holies; I am connected and bound to things that are worthwhile.

The dance was winding down. It was time for me to fearlessly assume the direction of my own life and make choices based on listening to the inner voice and being bound to the loving connections of creation, discernment, freedom, unconditional love and *creativity.*

The last night of my retreat I created another ritual. I broke bread and drank wine in gratitude and communion with the Creator and all of creation as the sun gently waned, and evening danced onto the vast stage of a darkening sky. I sat quietly in the stillness listening once more to the earth songs scurrying for comfort, letting my mind play back the music of all the nights of this extraordinary year. So many feelings surfaced, so mixed together that I felt vulnerable and mournful and thrilled and excited all at once.

There was grief for the ending of a time of life which I could never experience again. Yet there was joy knowing I would be reunited with my daughter and parents the next day and soon with the rest of my family and good friends. There was anticipation of what was coming next in my life's journey. The book I was writing about the patterns of the feminine soul as personified by several women of the New Testament was well on its way to completion. And the sloe-eyed woman whose story has been languishing for 3000 years was showing up with greater frequency demanding to be heard. Truthfully, there was also a tiny twinge of anxiety over whether or not I would be able to hold onto living from the inside-out when I returned home.

The chorus of a song hummed through my head prompting me to get my guitar one last time. After all, what is a retreat without music? I grabbed the expensive song book I had recently berated myself for buying in California, and there it was. Singing softly to myself as I strummed, I inhaled the words and the promises.

Dance then, wherever you may be.
I am the Lord of the dance, said He;
And I'll lead you all, wherever you may be;
And I'll lead you all in the dance, said He.[13]

Listen, trust, act. Full circle. I crawled into bed and turned out the light while the images of the joyfully freeing Dance of Life faded into sleep. Hugging the promise of the song like a down blanket to my heart, I wanted to find out what new soul shaking adventures were waiting down the road *wherever I may be.*

Epilogue
Never the Same River Twice

You could not step twice into the same river;
for other waters are ever flowing on to you.
Heraclitus of Ephesus (540-480 BC)

After the goodbyes in Indiana, my daughter and I slowly wandered through eastern Kentucky where I was born, then east to the Skyline Drive in Virginia where we sampled the wineries and the Appalachian Trail. Bittersweet this time was as we shared the separation of the past year, both of us tentatively recognizing that we were on new ground. So sweet to have this gift of time and rediscover the closeness and intimacy that had always been a part of our relationship. Yet she, the child, was currently the settled one, the one who lived, worked and loved in her own home with her beloved. While I the mother, who had pulled up weeds and roots and glided on the wind, must now determine where and how to land. There in the late summer of my soul's journey, we were meeting for the first time as two grown women with two separate lives grounded in the soil of mutual love and respect. My daughter became the bridge I hadn't been aware I needed to cross-over from a time out of mind to the realities of returning to my old life.

"You can never step in the same river twice," Prof Noble lectured in Pre-Socratic Philosophy when I was a college sophomore. "That was Heraclitus' way of explaining that all is flux, that change is the immutable product of the constant upward and downward flow of all the elements, earth, air, fire, and water, of which everything is composed." I still remember how those words sank into my understanding.

That's so true! I remember thinking with the enthusiastic acceptance of youth. *We really can't step into the same river twice. The water is in constant motion even if it is calm and quiet. My feet will never step into the exact configuration a second time. The water has run on, the bottom mud and sand have shifted; the rocks and stones have worn down and tumbled.*

I reflected on Heraclitus from time to time over the years and his incandescent metaphoric reasoning. His words were comforting when the turmoil of inevitable changes and growth manifested in the ongoing cycles of living. Stepping into the river of our relationship, my daughter and I were both transformed by the power of time passing. From minute to minute none of us remains static, we are always in motion. Now was the time to deepen our commitment, our choice to remain current with one another's separate adult experiences and visions, becoming older and wiser together. Perhaps.

I left my woman-child at her new home in her chosen place, waving goodbye out the window of the Falcon until she disappeared from my rearview mirror. Finally, I was alone once more and heading back to where the journey began. Within a few hours I would greet sons and friends, house and familiar streets, a way of life that had also moved on while I was gone. What was awaiting me there?

The last rays of a late summer sun shocked the sky with the deep oranges and purples of the descending twilight. The tangy scent of salt water misted through the open window as I crossed back over the familiar Merrimac River almost one year to the day I left. I drove slowly up *my* street, laughing softly at how easily I slipped back into sounds of summer in a portside town, and how joyful the reunions of the evening to come would be. I chuckled as I passed the curb where I stood in dark and shivering dawns asking my inner voice if I should go right or left.

Parking the Falcon along a break-wall overlooking the peaceful bay where diehard windsurfers were catching the last breezes of the day, I closed my eyes. *You're not finished yet.* The words whispered up from the inside. If I had learned nothing else from the past year, I had learned to pay attention to words like these when they came from *that place.* I knew from the moment I crossed the bridge that the fizz was missing. That wonderful effervescence of spirit that had first shown up on a cold January night in my upper room was in retreat. That inside joyful affirmation that always presaged creativity and that I had learned to depend upon and trust had departed. So I sat quietly by the water as I had done so many times before, asking questions of the Spirit Within, hoping and praying that I had the courage to get it right.

"What did you do when you returned home?" people frequently ask.

"Well," I say, "the truth is I didn't." Sometimes I continue telling them that I did not go back to my old life as I had known it. I returned for a time while I reveled in the love of family and dear friends, but I knew in that deep unshakeable soul-place that I was not finished.

"Of course I'm unfinished," I said out-loud to myself. "Aren't we all?" Yet this was something more than understanding that none of us is finished in our life until we stop breathing. There was an urgency about the message, an unrelenting knowledge that I could not step in the same river twice. Something deep had shifted and I was no longer called to fit into the old life I had left the year before. I could not go back to living in reaction to outside voices. I needed to figure out how to do the last third of my life living into the creative, to continue experiencing the deep lessons of the soul.

Recently I was talking to a woman of mid-life, a nurse in the office where I was having a check-up, and she asked me what my book was about. After a brief description she said, "Boy, do I need to hear this! There is such a need for people to learn to trust their own inner spiritual voice. But," and here she looked a little anxious and sad at the same time, "all that change. Change is so hard. I'm not sure I could do it."

"Well," I tried to reassure her, "for me it was a long process. My inner voice did not require that I change everything overnight."

"But change is scary," she insisted.

"I know it is, especially when we are confronted with a choice. But don't we all change whether we're frightened or not?" I asked her. "If someone told me when I first got the idea to go camping for a year that I would not return to my life as it was at that moment, I would have run screaming in the opposite direction covering my ears."

Not everyone is called to do what I did. We are each called into relationship with the divine in the midst of our own uniqueness of self and circumstance. I also have a solid belief that we are all called to listen to our own inner voice and trust it to guide us through the changes of life that are inevitable. "For it must follow as night the day…" we are all riding on the winds of change. Why not risk making it a positive choice?

And so my life continues to be an exciting adventure of testing the waters of the ever-flowing river of God. The Falcon and I have long since parted company. In the fall, however, here in New England, when the air turns crisp and the sun shines a certain way on the changing leaves, I admit my heart does a little lurch of longing for that day I first took the road. Whenever I see a Falcon on the highway I feel a pang of loss.

The other side is, I have written two books, become a grandmother, led retreats and spent a year in an international school in Europe working for a graduate degree in Peace and Conflict Studies. What a year that was! It would take another book to tell all the stories and adventures of being the most *mature* student in the school. And so I try to live into each day taking all that I am, what I know, what I feel and integrating it into the present moment in order to give back to this world the gifts it has given to me. I have returned to what I saw and heard and felt when I was that three year old minister's daughter being noisy in church: "Feed my sheep."

My heartfelt prayer and wish for all of you is that you will take the risk of getting quiet and learn to listen to your inner voice, to trust what you hear, and act boldly on its guidance. I saw a movie the other day and at the very end one of the characters reminds himself and us, "Healing the universe comes from the inside." And the *Inner Voice* echoes, *Amen.*

Listen, listen, listen to my heart song
I will never forget you; I will never forsake you…

Notes

1. William Wordsworth, (1806), "The World is Too Much With Us." Paul Lieder, Robert Lovett, Robert Root, eds., *British Poetry and Prose,* 3rd Edition (Houghton Mifflin Company: Boston) 1950, p. 55

2. Psalm 46:10 *NRSV*

3. James 2: 26 *NRSV*

4. Thomas R. Kelly, (1941). *A Testament of Devotion* (HarperSanFancisco), 13.

5. Erik Erikson, (1963), "Eight Stages of Man," *Childhood and Society,* Second Edition (W.W. Norton & Sons: New York), 268.

6. Oliver Wendell Holmes, "The Chambered Nautilus," *Atlantic Monthly,* February, 1858

7. C. S. Lewis, (1942), *The Screwtape Letters,* (Mentor Edition: New American Library: New York and Scarborough, Ontario, 1988), 6-7

8. W.H.Auden, (1947), *The Age of Anxiety,* "Good Friday: Horae Canonicae," line 407.

9. R. L. Wing, Translator, (1986), *The Tao of Power: Lao Tsu's Classic Guide to Leadership, Influence and Excellence,* (Doubleday: New York, London, Toronto, Sydney, Auckland.)

10. English translation: *market, bakery, meat shop*

11. Thomas Merton, (1959), *Seeds of Contemplation,* (Dell Publishing Company, Inc.: 261 Fifth Avenue, New York 16, New York), 118

12. Kokopelli is the shape of the flute player with a rucksack on his back. His carved figure is seen throughout the Anasazi pueblo dwellings. Speculation has him as a man who traveled from one community to the next, perhaps as a traveling salesman, or as a sort of ambassador from as far away as Mexico. Whatever or whoever, he was one of this continent's early campers.

13. Sydney Carter, (1968), "Lord of the Dance," (Copyright: Galliard Ltd.; Galaxy Music Corporation, NY, the U.S. Agency).

Printed in the United States
63525LVS00005B/304-360